HOPE'S LAST HOME

Travels in Milk River Country

TONY REES

Johnson Gorman Publishers

THE PUBLISHERS

Johnson Gorman Publishers

Red Deer, Alberta, Canada

CREDITS

Cover Photo by Tom Willock

Cover and Text Design by Full Court Press Inc.

Printed and Bound in Canada by Webcom Limited for Johnson Gorman Publishers

ACKNOWLEDGMENTS

Financial support provided by the Alberta Foundation for the Arts, a beneficiary of the Lottery Fund of the Government of Alberta.

COMMITTED TO THE DEVELOPMENT OF CULTURE AND THE ARTS

CANADIAN CATALOGUING IN PUBLICATION DATA

Rees, Tony, 1948–

Hope's last home

ISBN 0-921835-32-9

1. Rees, Tony, 1948– 2. Milk River Region (Alta.)—Biography.
3. Milk River Region (Alta.)—Description and travel. I. Title

FC3695.M515R33 1995   971.23'4   C95-910514-X

F1079.M515R33 1995

This book is for my children,
David and Julia,
and for Donna,
who made it possible.

−TR

country: to the ranchers and farmers and government officials, to the store owners, bartenders and coffee shop waitresses on both sides of the Medicine Line who contributed immeasurably and often unknowingly to this enterprise.

A great debt of gratitude is owed to Roy and Christie Audet and to Charlie and Judy Barnett. The very embodiment of western hospitality, they invited me into their homes and were unfailingly generous with their time and knowledge. Special thanks to Dennis Milner and Tom Willock of Medicine Hat; to Art Rich of Babb, Montana; to Lavinia Henderson, Ken Brown and Paul Madge of the town of Milk River, and to the staff of Calgary's Glenbow Archives & Library.

To Chuck Stormes, my good friend and the best damned saddle maker anywhere: thank you for your encouragement, for your patience and, most important of all, for teaching me something about how to see.

Finally, this book owes its life to Donna Kynaston. Careful researcher, gentle critic, long-suffering listener and road-trip companion *par excellence*, her faith in me and in this work never wavered. Words are not enough!

A Note on the Text

This book has been written using the old Imperial/American measures: in acres, miles and pounds. Partly, it acknowledges the fact that even where it flows through Alberta, the Milk has always been primarily an American river. Mostly, though, it's because I've yet to meet a rancher or farmer who talks in hectares, kilometers or kilograms. Spellings for the names of the various First Nations also use the American form—the general term Blackfeet rather than Blackfoot, Piegan rather than Peigan—except where the context is clearly Canadian.

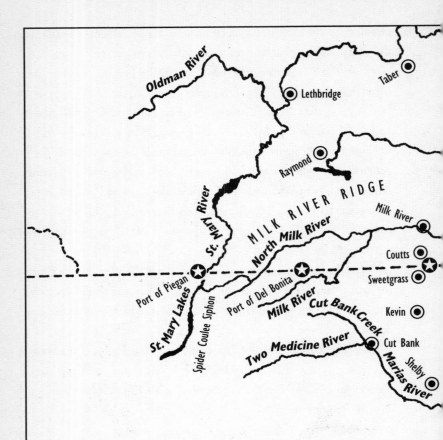

HOPE'S LAST HOME

Travels in Milk River Country

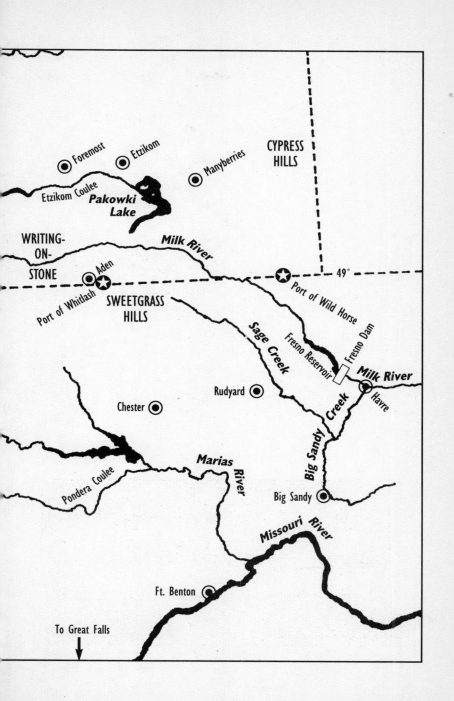

*One saw here the world as it had taken shape and
form from the hands of the Creator.*
—CAPTAIN W.F. BUTLER

THE
QUIET
EYE

n unmarked, unimproved gravel road meets Alberta's Highway 62 about halfway between the town of Magrath and the United States border at Del Bonita. The road cuts east and south along the shoulder of the Milk River Ridge for a couple of miles and ends in a shallow valley marked only by a spray of indefinite trails and tire track ruts.

There is nothing obviously remarkable in the geography of this shallow valley. Dozens more like it cut down from the rounded spine of the ridge, their eroded slopes scoured by the almost constant wind, their narrow, unnamed creeks filled only intermittently by spring runoff or summer downpour. Still there is something special here at the head of this valley. It would take a surveyor's transit to place it exactly and its almost intangible relief would be measured in inches rather than in thousands of feet, yet it is as authentic a barrier as the peaks of the Rocky Mountains rising sixty miles to the west. There is a continental divide running across the floor of Lonely Valley.

At the end of the gravel road, on the floor of the valley, two creeks rise within a few dozen yards of each other. One, unnamed and more often dry than not, cuts northwest, drops off the ridge to meet Pothole Creek at Jensen Reservoir and from there flows north into the St. Mary River below Lethbridge. The St. Mary joins its waters with the Oldman, which loops sharply east and north toward the South Saskatchewan, tracking the old fur trade routes back to Lake Winnipeg, the Great Lakes and Hudson Bay. Just yards away, Lonely Valley Creek falls away southeast. Picking up a few nameless tributaries along its ten miles of life, it comes off the ridge to lose itself in the North Milk River's Montana-born water. A few miles downstream, the North Milk meets the South, and their combined course is drawn steadily east by south, back across the 49th parallel and down to the Missouri and the Mississippi and eventually to the Gulf of Mexico below New Orleans. The Milk River country is the only part of Canada within the watershed of the Mississippi, and this gives the valleys and all the lands within the arc of the Milk a history unique in the Americas.

Some thirty straight-line miles to the southeast of the head of Lonely Valley, the town of Milk River is the first gas and coffee stop north of the border crossing between Sweetgrass, Montana, and Coutts, Alberta. With a population just under a thousand, Milk River is the only town—the only settlement at all—on three hundred miles of the river from its Blackfeet Reservation source against the Montana Rockies to the Hi-Line city of Havre.

At the south end of Milk River, welcoming the cars and trucks coming up from Interstate 15, eight different flags snap above the municipal campground. Faded by strong, constant sunlight and frayed by a relentless west wind, the flags display the history of this country from left to right: the gold fleurs-de-lis of Louis XIV, the castles and lions of Spain's Carlos IV, the *tricouleur* of Napoleonic France, the thirteen stripes and fifteen stars of Thomas Jefferson's United States, the standard of the Hudson's Bay Company, the Union Jack of the United Kingdom, the Red Ensign and the single Maple Leaf of Canada. First raised in 1967, the flags were the town's contribution to the celebration of one hundred years of Canadian confederation, the original of which would have passed utterly unnoticed by the few people, white or native, who happened to be in the vicinity at the time. Historians might quibble with the selection, with whether the Red Ensign and its Maple Leaf successor mark a distinction without a difference, but Milk River's claim to its special heritage is valid. At some time or another in the past three centuries, each of these standards waved in law if not in fact over the townsite and over the thousands of square miles of Canadian land drained by its namesake river.

I thought I already knew the history of this place, knew it in the way things were learned when history was still a subject taught every day from grade one to graduation. Years ago, I had connected the important names with the correct dates and wrapped them in something of the whys and wherefores, but the flags at Milk River still came as a surprise. Canada, I knew, was made by France and England, made by ancient battles high on cliffs above the St. Lawrence, by the Scots and the voyageurs racing toward the Rockies after beaver, by the railway and the settlers who rattled west along its endless, narrow track and poured out into every remote corner of this wide land. So what were the Spanish doing here, a thousand miles from their high southwestern deserts? When and why did the line between America and Canada once extend just these few miles above the

49th parallel? How did this place come to be the exception to the sagas in the high school history texts?

Sadly, for the storyteller, there are no great tales of heroic battles for the heart of the continent. Empires did not stand and fall in this remote quarter. The Milk River was not passed from hand to hand because it afforded some grand strategic advantage or because of the riches to be found here. The Milk River mattered only because of where its water went. It did not go the way Canada's western rivers are supposed to, the way all the others go: north and east toward Hudson Bay. Twelve thousand years ago, at some small place along its course across the northern plains, the river was turned south by a conspiracy of geology and the last great glacier, and connected with a history that would be different from the rest of the Canadian plains, tied to Old Louisiana, to Napoleon, Jefferson and the storied travels of Lewis and Clark.

I didn't set out to discover the spot where the European history of this country began. Rather, the place presented itself to me one cool morning in early summer when I parked on the shoulder of Highway 501 where it crosses Pakowki Lake. I had come to this place looking for birds, stopping along the way to scan the muddy shoreline of every small pothole and pond for the last of the migrants and the first of the nesters. Along with the rowdy flocks of marbled godwits and stately pairs of avocets, I was hoping for a glimpse of the black-necked stilts, which were sometimes reported hereabouts, looking for a chance to list a bird that the field guides call accidental this far north of its summer range in the Great Basin of Utah and Nevada.

All the maps show Pakowki Lake as just that: a lake, something with enough water in it to justify its blue ink outline. But here I was, on the floor of a wide, shallow swale, surrounded by greening grass and fence wire, stared at by white-faced cattle grazing where the water was supposed to be. Spread across the hood of the truck, pinned against the steady wind by binoculars and bird books, the 1:50,000 topographic map matched the view of the broad valley bottom stretching away to the southeast, running smooth as a tabletop down to the Milk River.

The map does not name this grand corridor, but local histories call it Pendant d'Oreille Coulee. Four or five miles below Highway 501, the Milk River flows east past the broad mouth of the Pendant d'Oreille, sweeping back and forth across its flat, graveled bed in a series of meanders. It looks as if it wants to turn up the coulee and follow the natural tilt of the land toward the north, but at the last moment it swings back toward the southeast.

Above the broad confluence, from the rim of the valley, the eye cannot discern the subtle rise which must lie somewhere across the mouth of the coulee. It is the same imperceptible divide that must have been here twelve thousand years ago, stopping a declining, glacial Milk from turning north to run through the network of meltwater channels that lace the land all the way up to the South Saskatchewan. The dry gravels of the Pendant d'Oreille estuary mark the last place where the river might have broken out of its shallow valley. Below the coulee, the Milk snakes away into the spectacular canyon which sealed its fate as a Missouri river. Thousands of years later and thousands of miles away, the small geological fact of this place would begin to matter.

On April 9, 1682, René-Robert Cavelier de La Salle gave Milk River its first flag, raising the three gold fleurs-de-lis of Louis XIV over the broad, muddy flats of the Mississippi

Delta over two thousand miles away. As he did, he claimed for his king, not just the great river itself, but "all the nations, peoples, provinces, cities, towns, villages, mines, minerals, fisheries, streams and rivers comprised." In short, he claimed the whole heart of the North American continent. In this one grandiloquent absurdity, La Salle not only defined the full extent of the French Empire in North America, but also gave voice to the wonderful fantasies which were the sum of European knowledge of the lands stretching away, beyond even their wild imagining, to the north and west.

But it was not the North and West which interested either him or his Sun King. What La Salle was after was what he had right in front of him: the brackish plane of the delta and control of the place where the Mississippi meets the sea, the place where New Orleans would grow to be the crown of his Louisiana.

He could not have understood in any real sense the breadth of what he had claimed, but he grasped the enormous strategic value which the mouth of the Mississippi possessed. In one bold stroke he had driven a wedge between the Spanish colonies of Florida and Mexico, establishing a link between New France far to the north and King Louis' Caribbean hopes, and in declaring the full length of the Mississippi to be a French waterway, he effectively foreclosed on any ambitions Britain's American colonies may have held for the country west of the Alleghenies. His claim on the West—on its supposed nations, peoples, provinces and cities—was a claim on a country most of which no European had then seen. Still, by blind luck, not careful diplomacy, it was a claim on the strength of a flag and a prayer which tidily finished the imperial division of North America east of the Great Divide. La Salle's claim to all the waters which drained into the Mississippi, including the Missouri and, had he known it, the Milk, filled what the European mind saw as a vacuum between the Spanish and British presence on the continent.

The peripatetic Spaniards had been circling north and east out of New Mexico for nearly 150 years before La Salle's grand gesture. But theirs was a listless wandering, driven by steadily eroding hopes for still unpillaged cities of gold, and it brought them nowhere near this northern shoulder of the Great Plains. Increasingly disconnected from the heart of an empire already well past middle age, the successors to Columbus were hardly in a position to challenge the French stake on their northern boundaries, even had they wanted to.

Twelve years before La Salle's small ceremony on the great delta, England's Charles II had by proxy formalized an equally sweeping and equally vague claim to all the lands which drained from the eastern slope of the Rocky Mountains into Hudson Bay. His grant of a fur trade monopoly to the Hudson's Bay Company in what he called Rupert's Land presupposed that such lands were his to give and, though he excluded from his generosity those places which might already be "possessed by the Subjectes of any other Christian Prince or State" (aboriginals excluded), the Hudson's Bay Company, in right of its king, now claimed the north flank of New France and extended it almost across the continent.

At the ragged, undefined edge of their new world, British and French claims to the immense heart of the continent met and ended in a narrow triangle in the shadow of the mountains high on the Milk River Ridge. It would take more than another century, in a time when France's presence in North America had been extinguished once and for all, before the true dimensions of those two vast watershed empires were known. More than another century would pass before the alloy of hope, rumor and outright fantasy was replaced by the cold, irrefutable fact of the sextant, the notebook and the practiced eye. By then, though, the *primum mobile* of the British and French—the prime beaver pelt—would be heading for a fall, a victim of changing fashion and the industrial revolution. By the time the great powers knew the full extent of what they had claimed, they had almost ceased caring about most of it, and in only a few decades both Britain and Spain would join the French in seeking their fortunes elsewhere.

Before they left, though, the three empires played their great game to its logical end. Eventually, their declining hopes for the perpetual wealth of silver and fur dulled their passion for the land itself, and they began to view the boundless horizons west of their permanent settlements less as an opportunity and more as an obstacle standing between them, the Pacific and the shortcut to the fast money of the China trade. The emerging truths about their vast lands steadily and surely put final flight to dreams of a great inland sea, a river of the West, a short, low portage to the Pacific, the Seven Cities of Gold and just about every other fantasy that had made it all seem worthwhile.

La Salle at least harbored some hope for actually colonizing and developing his piece of the West. He saw, in the fertile valleys of the Mississippi and its tributaries, sufficient land of sufficient quality to feed both New France and the sugar islands, lands which could grow rich on the profits of the trade with both, while remaining invulnerable to the external forces which could isolate and starve New France by choking off the mouth of the St. Lawrence. His vision was of villages of

French men and women, not of converted heathens, but there were never sufficient resources or enough serious interest forthcoming from France, and fur continued to represent eighty percent of the wealth of French North America. Even La Salle, always a source for wild schemes and hopeless speculation, soon gave up on his utopia, opting instead for an invasion of Spanish New Mexico. The get-rich-quick scheme never had a chance, La Salle was assassinated by what was left of his company and the beaver trade remained the chief preoccupation of the French on the upper Mississippi.

For Britain, the general policy seemed to be one of exploitation rather than of conquest. The natives' trading networks were too valuable to be disrupted by the hard sell invasion approach. The key to success in the Northwest was to be pure business without the interference of priests and other evangelical do-gooders. The Hudson's Bay Company posts were there to slip a new factor into the trade equation, not to rewrite it. Where the native trade had been in furs and food and shells and pipestone, now it would be in furs and pots and muskets and beads, with the Company steadily siphoning off more than it put in. And the policy worked like a charm, more or less, for nearly two hundred years.

Spain, too, had always been willing to trade with the natives who lived within her sphere of influence, but it was always the same hard bargain: Spanish Christianity for the natives' gold and silver. There was nothing else on offer. Their hold on the lands north of Old Mexico seemed always tenuous at best, and at the end of the seventeenth century, the original residents tired of the bargain and actually drove them out (and kept them out for twelve years). While the Spaniards were comfortable in the semiarid and pure desert country of New Mexi-

co, those who first confronted the horizon-stretching grasslands of the interior plains always seemed more befuddled than
inspired. While they kept nicely detailed accounts of where
they had been and what they had seen, they were always looking over their shoulders, wondering if they could circle back to
New Mexico before winter or some other calamity befell them.
How wildly inappropriate then that the flag of Spain should be
the second of eight to wave over the Milk River.

How Spain came to possess something which she never
really seemed to want turned not on the axis of the western
lands themselves, but on yet another convulsive reordering of
Europe. When the Seven Years War ended in 1760, the map of
North America, inaccurate and incomplete as it was, had
changed dramatically. With the fall of Quebec, France was
gone. The Treaty of Paris defined the new order and gave
Britain unquestioned dominion over the whole continent from
Florida (gained from Spain in exchange for Cuba) to the Arctic
and west to the Rocky Mountains. Her American colonies had
finally broken over the Alleghenies and now stretched from the
Atlantic to the east bank of the Mississippi. But they could go
no farther west.

Though the French could not hold the eastern half of La
Salle's claim, they weren't prepared to quit the continent without
one final slap at the British. In 1860, knowing Quebec and most
of the rest were lost, they hedged their bets on the future, exe-
cuted a secret treaty with the Spanish and handed them not only
the three thousand square miles around New Orleans, but everything else west of the river which had been their Louisiana.
When the victors sat down in 1763 to divide their spoils, the
Missouri, the Yellowstone, the Musselshell and the Milk were
not on the table. If they could not be French, then at least they

would not be British, and the Milk River country had Spain for its second absentee landlord.

While the Treaty of Paris effectively knocked France out of the imperial equation in North America, it also started the clock ticking on the time which Britain and Spain would have to enjoy their new lands. The inheritors of French dreams of empire below the Great Lakes would be neither the Spanish nor the British—they would be the Americans, and before the eighteenth century was out the new United States had brought its own imperial aspirations to the banks of the Mississippi. No one believed for a minute, least of all the Americans, that either the river or its Spanish guardians could keep them from the Pacific and from final possession of all the lands they would cross to reach it.

The Americans were unique among the empire builders in that they did not see the West as a simple source of wealth, a shorter passage to China or a fruitful ground for religious conversion. They saw it as theirs by natural right, and they saw it as a logical extension of the agrarian Eden they had carved out of the wilderness along the Atlantic coast. To the Americans, the Mississippi and its tributaries were not great boundaries or sensible borders between nations. They were highways meant for the distribution of their new wealth throughout a new nation and via New Orleans to the sugar islands of the Caribbean and anywhere else in the wide world they wanted to go. But first, they needed New Orleans, and it would take another war in Europe and the brief return of France to get it for them.

In 1800, Napoleon Bonaparte brought France back to North America. Perhaps the first man to perceive the world as a geopolitical whole, Bonaparte saw North America as he had seen Egypt: a crucial element in his war to break the British once and for all. In return for his regaining Louisiana, Napoleon offered the tired and declining Spanish King Carlos IV a new kingdom in Tuscany, and Carlos was no position to argue. It was the beginning of the end for the empire of Columbus and Cortés, and over the next twenty years or so, Spain would again and again be in no position to argue as one after another of its colonies in the Americas declared independence and made it stick.

Almost from the moment he had regained Louisiana, though, Napoleon realized it was not the trump card he needed. British naval power was great and would react swiftly and absolutely, as it had at Trafalgar, to any overseas threat he presented. The only way to strike a fatal blow against Britain was to strike at Britain herself. After she had fallen, all her colonies would be Bonaparte's for the taking, so he never really bothered to take Louisiana.

The United States, in its own way as imperialist as the rest and deeply troubled by the threat that France would return, had been trying for years to negotiate free access to the mouth of the Mississippi. They had gotten nowhere, the Europeans having other, more pressing things on their minds. It is hard to imagine, then, the shock in April 1803 when an American official in Paris arrived for his routine round of futile pleading for New Orleans and was asked, point-blank, what the United States would be willing to pay for everything. What would they pay for all of Louisiana?

Given speed-of-sail communications, word was so slow to reach the towns along the Mississippi that, at St. Louis, the three-way transfer had to be effected in just over twenty-four hours. Using whatever near-dignitaries could be rushed to the scene and mustering what little pomp and ceremony they could manage, the Spanish flag was lowered and the French *tricouleur* raised in its place, only to be replaced the next day by the Stars and Stripes.

With the stroke of a pen and the transfer of less than twelve million dollars, a twelve-year-old republic had more than doubled in size and now reached all the way to the Rocky Mountains. The Continental Divide would prove no more than a minor annoyance on the Americans' drive to the Pacific.

The Milk River had its third and fourth flags in the space of one day and still, in 120 years, none of its landlords had seen it or even known of its existence. Two years later, in May 1805, the new American owners had not only seen the river, but had given it a name and marked its lower course clearly on the map of the western lands. Eighteen months later, the travelers were back in St. Louis, having planted the American claim to the West firmly on the Pacific Coast. Eventually, the 49th parallel would be drawn across the western plains, and the northern arc of the Milk River would fall under control of the Hudson's Bay Company. Later, the territory would be joined to the new nation of Canada, and the Milk River country would have its last four flags.

The confused geology of the Rocky Mountain front created the Milk's elliptical watershed, and its shape, sketched on a map, describes a ragged, almond eye lidded by the tidy, unnatural precision of the 49th parallel. The image reflects perfectly the history of the Milk River country: the calm center of the huge geopolitical storms which swirled around it for the 150 years it took to settle the course of empire in North America and, in the century and a half since, the dispassionate observer of the boom-and-bust extremes which gave final shape to the Prairie West.

It was here in Milk River country that the last, vast continental glaciers stalled and began to die; here that the remnant buffalo, the prairie wolf and the plains grizzly waited out their final days. It was here that Sitting Bull and Little Soldier and Chief Joseph drew the final curtain on the brilliant horse cultures of the plains nations; here that cattlemen found their last free range and here that the fence-wired illusions of the last homesteaders dried up and blew away.

Driving across this country on a cloudless day in early summer, I could easily hear the pitches of the railway agents and the land speculators, easily imagine being taken in by their promises. The rains had been plentiful, as they were in those last land-rush springs before the Great War, and the country was rich with varied greens, cooled by a constant, easy breeze. Even with the clarity of hindsight, it was difficult to look beneath the lush veneer and see this beautiful land for what it has always been: a last place, a final frontier, a sere, indifferent swallower of dreams.

Hard to ford, destitute of fish, too dirty to bathe in and too thick to drink.

—AN ANONYMOUS EARLY SETTLER'S IMPRESSION
OF WESTERN RIVERS

ABOUT THE COLOR OF A CUP OF TEA

The northern tier of the high plains is Lewis and Clark country. Meriwether Lewis, the pale, thin-faced Virginian given to manic bouts of high energy and deep depression would die by his own hand in a fit of alcoholic despair only three years after reaching the Pacific. William Clark, the tall, red-headed Kentuckian, would go on to marry and name his son Meriwether, serve as Missouri's territorial governor and die in his bed in 1838 at the age of sixty-eight. As different in their manner as they were equal in their passion, they engineered one of the great triumphs of western exploration.

I am constantly surprised by the persistence of their legacy along the route to the Pacific. Their journals continue to be published in every sort of edition from huge, beautifully bound reproductions of the original diaries and maps to straightforward paperbacks which do the reader the favor of correcting their atrocious and thoroughly inconsistent spelling. There are serious tracts on their work as naturalists, and dozens of guide books take the modern traveler along their route from St. Louis, Missouri, to Astoria, Oregon, at the mouth of the Columbia.

Today, there are monuments to their epic passage everywhere across the northern tier. Through the Dakotas, Montana, Idaho and Washington, Lewis and Clark are remembered in the names of towns, highways, rivers and mountain ranges and ironically on the label of a better-than-average whiskey. The official Montana tourist map is covered with a veritable rash of tiny reproductions of the "official" Lewis and Clark logo: two men in profile, one in a Davy Crockett cap leaning on a musket, the other in a frock coat and cocked hat. Their exploits in this state alone rate a full panel on the back of the map.

Though so much has changed along the Missouri since their voyage of discovery in 1805—the unbroken string of massive dams, the sprawling cities and intensive, high-tech agriculture—there are still a precious few lonely places where the river remains as they first saw it, wild and untouched. Down in the Missouri Breaks below Fort Benton, I have seen landmarks which Lewis and Clark described and which can still be recognized from the work of the early watercolorists who followed on their heels within a decade or so. Most of the animals they were the first to describe and collect have disappeared forever from the plains—the grizzly, the big horn sheep and mountain goats—but the captains' memory survives. It lives on in Lewis's woodpecker and Clark's nutcracker, in Montana's state fish, the cutthroat trout *(Oncorhynchus clarki lewisi)* and in the state flower, the bitterroot. Its Latin name, *Lewisia rediviva*, translates into the delightful "Lewis come back to life."

The question of exactly what Lewis and Clark were doing

on the upper Missouri is intriguing since the conception for their grand exercise had been born in times far less settled than those which prevailed in the spring of 1805.

The Lewis and Clark expedition was the creation of Thomas Jefferson. Well before the French had offered Louisiana for sale (indeed well before it was even theirs to sell), Jefferson had included it in his idea of what the new United States logically and naturally encompassed. As United States minister to the court of Louis XVI from 1784 to 1789, Jefferson had begun to acquire books on western North America and, it is said, ended up owning more of them than any other collector in the world (though he would never get farther west than fifty miles from his Virginia plantation). Between the end of the American Revolution and 1800, he had seen the American population west of the Alleghenies grow from thirty thousand to ten times that number, and he knew the Spanish could not stop the flood across the river. Nor honestly could he see why they should be allowed to.

In 1801, almost as soon as he had been elected to his first term, President Jefferson moved to bring American aspirations to bear on the worldwide events which were then swirling about it. If Spain had actually retroceded Louisiana to the French, would it provoke a British strike at New Orleans? Would France or, worse, Britain replace the impotent Spanish as the barrier across the Mississippi? Could Alexander Mackenzie convince the British to create a new and sweeping western trade monopoly to manage not only the lands he had crossed on his way to the Pacific, but also the upper Missouri and the still disputed Oregon territories?

Believing that none of these possibilities would be realized for several years, Jefferson undertook to learn as much as he could about the still murky regions which lay between the Mississippi and the Pacific. His principal agent for such a reconnaissance would be a small, mobile force disguised, as expediency and local conditions dictated, as either a scientific or trade mission. To set the plan in motion, he turned to his new private secretary, Meriwether Lewis.

All the talk about commerce and science was far from being entirely a smoke screen. Jefferson was keenly interested in the wonders of nature, especially those which he assumed lay to the west. A longtime member of the American Philosophical Society, Jefferson was a most singular product of the Enlightenment, believing the universe to be a rational, ordered place. He was fascinated by the natural world and man's place in it, and he had a vision for his America which extended far beyond the rape-and-pillage boosterism and get-rich-quick schemes which were so much a part of the western landscape. His vision for America was Arcadian; he saw the West as a civilized place, an extension of the coastal settlements which surrounded him. The promulgation of that dream, he knew, would depend upon hard knowledge of the place, and at the end of the eighteenth century, there was precious little of that.

Lewis was sent on a series of crash courses in botany, zoology, astronomy, surveying, cartography and ethnology, and Jefferson saw to it that he would have the latest maps and as thorough an understanding as possible about the political state of the world as it bore on the western lands.

Commerce would be the engine of western development, providing the initial settlements, building the transportation routes and generally preparing the way for the yeomen farmers and planters who Jefferson seemed to believe would come to constitute the real wealth of the West. When Jefferson thought of commerce, he still thought of furs, but the list of discoveries which had accumulated over the previous decades had dramatically changed American and European attitudes toward trade and the role it ultimately could play.

When Scottish explorer Alexander Mackenzie had set out to cross the continent for the British in 1789, he had ended up tasting salt water, but it was the Arctic Ocean he found, not the Pacific. He had paddled down the huge, fast river that now bears his name, looking always for it to turn west and cut through the enormous mountain barriers which were constantly to his left. The ranges never broke and Mackenzie knew then that there was no broad, easy passage to the Western Sea. Jefferson knew it, too.

Accepting that any route to the Pacific would have to include an overland portion, Jefferson still expected it to be a short and convenient one. After all, when Mackenzie finally got it right in 1793, his traverse of the Great Divide had been over a low ridge between two small lakes, a distance he carefully reported as being exactly 817 paces. The Spanish, decades before, had found their crossing even easier, but no one knew the nature of the barrier between the Missouri and the Columbia.

The staking of American and European (and even Russian) ambition on the Pacific was already well advanced. James Cook, on his voyage up the coast in 1788, had seen, in the hands of the natives, iron and copper and brass—manufactured goods, he correctly surmised, which must have come overland through a native trading network from some distant Hudson's Bay Company post.

In 1792, the voyages of George Vancouver's *Discovery* and American Robert Gray's *Columbia* had established clearly where the Great River of the West poured into the Pacific. On Gray's previous voyage in 1789–90, he had left the West Coast with a stock of sea otter pelts, traded them in China for a cargo of tea and returned to Boston around the Cape of Good Hope, incidentally becoming the first American to circumnavigate the globe. Vancouver, continuing his meticulous way north up the coast in 1793, missed by only six weeks the sight of a battered Alexander Mackenzie paddling toward him down the Dean Channel, coming, as the Scotsman famously wrote on a seaside rock, "From Canada, By Land."

Mackenzie and Jefferson likely came upon their concept of a new West independently, but the American publication of the Scot's account of his travels to the Pacific gave a new urgency to the Americans' expeditionary plans. Mackenzie had clearly articulated what he thought should be the British strategy in the West. Goods from the East would move across the continent, and the furs they were traded for would be sent both east and west, to Europe or China. Silk and tea and huge profits from the sea otter trade with China would come east from settlements on the coast, some traded along the way, most bound for Montreal or Europe. The 49th parallel would be out, replaced by an international boundary enforced at 45° north, giving Britain clear title to the Columbia, the upper Missouri and just about everything else which really mattered.

For Jefferson, some obvious differences acknowledged, the vision was the same. The center of the continent would be the center of commerce, but the furs and silks and pots and guns would move between the Columbia and New Orleans or New York, not Montreal, and they would move on the Missouri, not on the Saskatchewan.

The question of boundaries was crucial to Jefferson's dreams for the West because no one really knew where the boundaries were. Indeed, in 1805, they really weren't anywhere at all. The Louisiana Purchase had given the United States all of French North America that was not already British or Spanish, though it had never been clearly established what that was (or wasn't).

On the northern plains, two major factors underpinned the debate about boundaries. First were the watersheds. Britain's Rupert's Land was a watershed, as was La Salle's Louisiana. After the Treaty of Paris, Spanish Louisiana had been reduced to those lands which lay to the west of the Mississippi. The obvious problem was that almost no one had seen much of that country, and most of those who had were wonderfully (and sometimes deliberately) uncertain about exactly where they had been.

The second element was the 49th parallel. The idea of an arbitrary line between what had been competing British and French interests grew from the Treaty of Utrecht in 1713. In seeking to establish clearly who owned the beaver, the treaty suggested a westward extension of the boundary between what are now Ontario and Minnesota. It may have seemed logical to someone sitting in a European palace, but it wasn't to anyone who had even the remotest notion of what lay west of Lake-of-the-Woods (and a remote notion was about all that anyone had).

While later politicians and diplomats were well aware of the treaty, their arguments about it were pure expedience. Did the 49th parallel clause apply to lands which were no longer French? That depended on whether the various prevailing national wisdoms felt that they would gain more by the parallel than they would by the watershed. Interestingly, the argument was moot. The Treaty of Utrecht did not mandate the 49th parallel—it only suggested the line as a solution, leaving the final decision to a commission. And the commission never actually got around to talking about it.

Jefferson was well acquainted with the treaty, as his instructions to Lewis and Clark made clear, and he, too, was hedging his bets on which definition of Louisiana—parallel or watershed—he was willing to accept. It mattered. There were crucial questions which had to be answered. What was the true latitude of the source of the Mississippi? How far north did the Missouri wander before it turned south and west into the mountains? How close to the Saskatchewan did the Missouri or its tributaries really come? What about the Red and the Souris rivers, and most important of all, what about the Columbia?

When all the planning and secretive scheming was taking place, Louisiana was still not an American possession. But by the time the Corps of Discovery was ready to move into the West, the West was theirs, the result, it seems, of kismet rather than hard diplomacy.

As Lewis and Clark and their Corps of Discovery paddled and man-hauled their way up the Missouri in the spring of 1805, their principal goal was to reach the Pacific via the Great River of the West. Within a few days of leaving their overwintering site at the Mandan villages in present-day North Dakota, they would be in territory which no white man had ever visited. The course of the upper Missouri represented the last substantial block of North America still unseen and largely unknown to white explorers, but it could hardly be described as *terra incognita.*

The Spanish had wandered through most of the country to the south, crossing the continent regularly between Texas and California via their ancient holdings around Santa Fe. Between

1760 and 1776, they had followed the Colorado River nearly to its source and seen the Great Salt Lake of northern Utah. First French, then American traders, trappers and entrepreneurs had been striking west toward the silver-rich Spanish from the Mississippi and the lower Missouri, establishing posts along the Platte, the Arkansas and the other navigable tributaries.

During the winter of 1804–05, Lewis and Clark's Corps of Discovery had enjoyed the company of both British and French traders, some of them permanent residents, whose routes onto the central plains had been via the Souris and the Red, both of which drained north and fell within the domain of the Hudson's Bay Company. Agents for the Company and for the competing Nor'Westers had traveled, trapped and mapped the lands on either side of the Saskatchewan River for years, and their contacts with the Lewis and Clark's Mandan hosts dated back perhaps two decades.

So the Americans were well aware that their overland voyage to the Pacific would not be the first. The maps prepared for Lewis and Clark by Thomas Jefferson's cartographers included what had been learned from the Spanish and from Mackenzie's account of his trip to the Pacific (copies of which had appeared in Philadelphia in 1802), but also the exact location of their ultimate goal, the mouth of the Columbia, which had been reached from the sea by Robert Gray. Taking Gray's readings together with Nor'Wester David Thompson's close-to-exact longitude for the Mandan villages, a precise, straight-line distance across the unknown territory could be established. In other words, the Corps of Discovery was not sent marching off the edge of the known world. Rather, it set out to traverse, define and conquer an uncertainty between two knowns.

Before leaving the Mandan villages, the captains also had

drawn on the knowledge of the Mandan and their close allies, the Hidatsa. In the early going, their information was unerring. The huge, stately Yellowstone rolled in from the southwest just where the Hidatsa had said it would, though for the captains, the Hidatsa's descriptions did not do the river justice.

A few miles before reaching the Yellowstone, they had seen and added to their map what the Hidatsa had called *Ok-hah, Ah-zhah*, the White Earth River. The Indians had said this river led north, navigable almost as far as the South Saskatchewan. Though Lewis and Clark's prime directive was to reach the Pacific, one instruction among many from President Jefferson was to make careful record of any tributary to the Missouri which looked like it might give the Americans access to the long-established fur trade routes of the Hudson's Bay and North West companies. It was in the cause of commerce that Lewis and Clark explored the White Earth River for a few miles above its mouth, noting its white-stained alkaline banks and its muddy bottom. In a rare expression of wishful thinking, they saw in this stream, almost sixty yards wide near its confluence, some real promise of access to the Saskatchewan River country.

If the Hidatsa were right (and they had been so far) there was another, larger northern tributary to come. This was to be *Ah-mah-tah, Ru-shush-sher*, The River That Scolds At All Others. On May 8, much to their surprise, the Corps reached the scolding river. That the river existed, that it flowed from the north and that it was big, as the Hidatsa had claimed, was not surprising. Its location *was*.

Though the Hidatsa spoke of distance in terms of "sleeps," or how far a mounted rider could travel before sunset, the captains thought they had been able to translate such relative measures into miles. So far, their conversions had proved reliable. Now here was the scolding river, more than a hundred miles closer to the Yellowstone than it should have been. Such an error was of more than passing concern.

The scolding river was supposed to be close to the great falls of the Missouri, just upstream from where it turned from north to east. South of the great falls were the three forks which marked the Missouri's beginning. The westernmost of these was to take them up to the divide and a short portage to the Columbia. Lewis and Clark had made clear estimates of the distances between each of the major landmarks, and these told them they could cross the divide and make the Pacific before another winter set in. With their limited supplies, one mistake of a hundred miles could be compensated for; any more than that and they would be in trouble. The Corps would be a month farther up the Missouri before the dangerous puzzle was solved.

Their travel upstream from the scolding river took them through what was to that point the most wildly impressive scenery they had encountered. The sublime canyons and spectacular eroded strata of what are now called the Missouri Breaks inspired Lewis's journal entries to poetic heights. The scenery could at least take their minds off the fact that the river had grown swifter and more shallow, the game more scarce and the spring creeks either too dry or too alkaline to drink.

If they or the Hidatsa had been wrong about the scolding river, the captains must have taken some comfort on May 20 as the Musselshell, the last southern tributary before the falls, appeared exactly where the Hidatsa said. And though they could not explain the premature appearance of the snow-capped peaks visible to the north and south, the mountains at least told them they were slowly and steadily coming up off the plains.

On June 2, they had another reason to doubt the Hidatsa. That doubt came in the form of what seemed to be a fork in the Missouri. They had made the final turn and were headed clearly southwest when the river divided. The steady, muddy waters they had been paddling carried on ahead, but turned more west than south. A large, clear, stone-bedded stream came rolling in on what should have been their course.

They had left the scolding river almost with a shrug, knowing it was the Missouri which they were to travel. This new dilemma could not be so easily resolved since they now faced the problem of having to decide which of two equal options was the Missouri. Most of the Corps was convinced that the muddy right-hand fork was the one. Though the smaller of the two, it was coming east toward them out of the mountains and looked exactly like the brownish soup through which they had pulled and poled their way for months.

Lewis and Clark looked at the same water and drew the opposite conclusion, their faith in the Hidatsa rattled but not yet broken. If, they reasoned, the true forks of the Missouri lay to the south, beyond the great falls, then the western river could not be correct. And its muddy water said it had obviously traveled a good while over the plains. The Hidatsa's estimate of the Corps' distance from the mountains meant the Missouri should, by now, look more like a mountain stream: clear and cold.

It was crucial that they get the right river. The success of the expedition, not to mention their very lives, depended on it, and since neither captain was prepared to dismiss the reasoning of their seasoned colleagues, it was decided, for the first time since leaving St. Louis, to divide the Corps and explore enough of both streams to determine which was the Missouri. Leaving seventeen men in camp to replenish the food supplies and repair the equipment, Clark took his party up the clear fork while Lewis started up the muddy.

Within two days Clark knew he had been right. The southern stream stayed clear and steady on its course, headed toward the falls, the forks and the divide. It took Lewis only one day longer to come to the same conclusion as the muddy stream he was following turned sharply north, paralleling, not approaching, the great ranges they had seen palisading the western horizon. Their men were still unconvinced, but the decision for the south fork was firm. Ironically, had Clark stayed out just one more day, he would have removed all doubt. One more day of travel and he would have heard the unmistakable roar of the great falls.

If the clear fork was the Missouri, then what was the muddy stream? The captains were quick to reason it out. The Hidatsa were horsemen. When they traveled for long distances across the broad, flat plains, they took the path of least resistance, moving in a straight line and ignoring the meandering rivers unless they had to ford them. Their raiding road to Shoshone country took them below the Missouri as it arched across the plains, and it joined the river near the great falls before moving up to the divide. The new muddy stream had to be the *Ah-mah-tah*, the real scolding river, and as had so often been the case, it was just where the Hidatsa had said it would be. The reason they had not mentioned the big northern tributary which had so worried and confused the Corps was simple: in crossing the country south of the Missouri, the Hidatsa had never seen it. With their confusion resolved and at least three sound possibilities for access to the British West added to their map, Lewis and Clark pushed on toward the Great Divide.

The more I read of their works and exploits, the more I travel their Missouri River country, the more I come to like Lewis and Clark. Always open and honest about their thoughts and feelings, perpetually curious about the new land and above all unwavering in their drive to accomplish their one great goal, they seem to me to represent the best of the Enlightenment. It's easy to point to the horrors which followed so quickly in their footsteps, to the murder and mayhem and whiskey and smallpox which took barely a generation to destroy the great buffalo cultures, but they were not of the captains' making. Save one fatal miscalculation among the Blackfeet, they passed across the northern plains and over the Great Divide having caused barely a ripple. They left no physical sign that they had been here at all except for William Clark's signature scratched into the soft sandstones at Pompey's Pillar down on the Yellowstone.

The fate of the Great Plains native cultures and the land on which they lived had been sealed years before Lewis and Clark came up the river to take their measure. It was inevitable from the moment the Spaniards colonized the southern deserts, the Hudson's Bay traders built their first factories or the Pilgrims landed at Plymouth Rock. The captains opened the way into the last unknown, and we are fortunate in Jefferson's choice of these two very particular individuals. With their maps and journals and collections of plants and animals, they created a wonderfully detailed record of what would all too soon become a lost world.

As pervasive a presence as Lewis and Clark remain across the Dakotas, Montana and the lands beyond the divide, they

rate barely a mention north of the 49th parallel. Though acute-
ly aware of the British presence on their northern flank, they
had no time to venture from the valleys and canyons of the
Missouri River basin and see these northern lands for themselves. As a consequence, their contribution to the history and
the maps of Canada is limited to just a single reference.

Far upstream from the great falls, at what was first believed
to be the Hidatsa's scolding river, the wind blew harder against
them than it usually did, and the Corps of Discovery paused
for more of its habitual reconnoitering. From a peak, Clark
believed he could see fifty or sixty miles upstream. "Level and
beautiful," he wrote. "It must water a large extent of country."
He saw that the river forked, the main branch trending to the
northwest but with a substantial stream coming straight south
toward him. "Perhaps," he recorded, mindful always of Jefferson, "this river also might furnish a practicable and advanta-
geous communication with the Saskashiwan River."

While careful and critical interpreters of everything they
saw, Lewis and Clark time and again give strong evidence in
their journals that they did not grasp something fundamental
about plains rivers and plains water in general. Their travels
across the northern plateau were in early spring when every living thing experiences explosive growth. Between the brutal winter's strength-sapping privation and the unrelenting heat of the
summer, there is one brief period of plenty. What was true for
the grasses, the buffalo and the beaver, however, was also true
for the rivers. The runoff of melting snow was their prime
source of water, and few were fed by the springs or lakes which
characterized the eastern rivers along which the captains had
lived all their lives. And spring came later to the plains than to
the coast, much later than it did to Virginia. In April and May,

even well into June, the western rivers were filled to the brim, but by August they could be almost dry. It was April 21 when Lewis and Clark had explored the White Earth River and proclaimed it a navigable route to the Saskatchewan. Later travelers, seeing it after the runoff, gave it another, more realistic name: Big Muddy Creek.

Lewis and Clark made the same mistake about this first scolding river. The right-hand fork which seemed to offer such promise of commerce with the North did not reach as far as its full, swift flow suggested. What is known today as Porcupine Creek is perhaps only forty miles long, rises well south of the international boundary and one hundred miles or more below the Saskatchewan.

The captains didn't care much for what they believed was the river's Indian name—*Ah-mah-tah, Ru-shush-sher*—and, observing it to be "about the color of a cup of tea with the admixture of a tablespoonful of milk," they rechristened it accordingly. They called it the Milk River.

In nature there are neither rewards nor punishments—
there are consequences.
—ROBERT GREEN INGERSOLL

AWFULLY DRY— NOT EVEN GREEN GRASS

T he prairies, the Prairie West, the prairie provinces—
Canadians call the lands between the Great Shield and
the Great Divide prairie, and it's an odd term for a
region that contains almost no prairie at all.

If there is—or was—a piece of true prairie in the Prairie
West, it is far to the east of the Milk River country, contained
within a rough triangle bounded on the south by the U.S. border, on the west by the 100th meridian running north through
Brandon, Manitoba, and by the arc of the shield back down to
the 49th parallel.

But for that small triangle of true prairie, the prairie
provinces—the Canadian plains—encompass two distinct
areas, the boundary between them blurred across a transitional
zone where the characteristics of both blend into something
that is itself unique. The northern half of the prairie provinces,
an area defined by the huge, convex curve of the Great Shield,
begins in Ontario at Lake-of-the-Woods and diagonals north

and west along the line punctuated by the great interior Lakes Winnipeg, la Ronge, Athabasca and Great Slave. This land is the visible extension of the great Canadian Shield, the true-north-strong-and-free landscape of Ontario, Quebec and the Group of Seven.

To the south and west, across the transitional zone of aspen parkland, lies the country which most Canadians see in their mind's eye when they think of prairie: the dry, flat infinity which marks the upper limits of the great North American plains. In their geology and climate, in their natural and human history, the Canadian plains share little with the shield country. In all these things, the city of Calgary, Alberta, has more in common with Denver, Colorado, or even Bismarck, North Dakota, than it does with Edmonton, fewer than two hundred miles to the north. The southern prairie provinces have a look, a sound and a "feel" that is more American than any other region of Canada, and the reasons for it run deeper than the obvious seductions of cattle and cowboys.

Walter Prescott Webb's seminal 1931 study, *The Great Plains*, is part history, part science and part consummate cautionary tale. In it, Webb defines the combination of elements unique to the plains environment: "The plains are flat, they are treeless and they are dry." Within the huge compass of this continental heartland, these elements may exist in various combinations and in varying degrees, but wherever any two appear, they make the Great Plains. Along the Milk River, all three are present in their purest form.

The plains are flat. The surface of the plains, seen against the lands of eastern and extreme western North America, is as level as a tabletop, a tabletop which slopes slightly but steadily toward the east. In Canada, the plains end at the Manitoba–Ontario border, where their bottomless sediments and glacial rubble wash up against the Precambrian hard rock of the great shield. To the west, the plains end in a series of high, flat intermountain valleys extending well beyond the Rockies' front ranges to where the Pacific slope begins its short, sharp drop to the sea. Kamloops, in the British Columbia interior, is a plains city and shares nothing but a time zone and an area code with coastal Vancouver.

In America, the plains begin at the base of the ancient Appalachians, extend across the full breadth of the continent as far as the Rocky Mountains, and in a series of plateaus and basins between the ranges, out to the Pacific slope. North to south, they run unbroken from the 49th parallel until they disappear under the shallow salt water of the Gulf of Mexico.

The plains are treeless. West of the Mississippi, there is simply not enough moisture to support serious timber. What there is grows on the wetter bottomlands along the rivers or on the flanks of the mountain ranges, but, as a percentage of the whole huge area, forests are but a scattering of islands in a boundless sea of grass. As well, trees grow slowly and root deeply, doing most of their work well above the ground, their leaves and branches too exposed to the extremes of temperature and the effects of fire. They simply cannot compete with the grasses, the plains' perfect tenants.

Yet in an era when we are obsessed with the loss of our trees, fighting over clear-cutting and the burning of the rain forest, recycling our paper to starve the voracious pulp mills, the high plains show more trees against their endless horizons than at any time since the grasses first colonized them. But this represents no change in the harsh environment, no softening of the hard rules. The trees are here because people do not like to

live without them. Look at the old photographs, the turn-of-
the-century images of the great open range before the homesteaders came, and it's easy to see why something as simple as
scrounging a few sticks for a cooking fire was worthy of note in
the journals of the earliest travelers.

Men and women brought trees into this country, planting
them in regular rows around their homeplaces to break the
incessant winds and shade their houses from the endless beat-
ing of the sun. Some may have tried to transplant precious
shoots of the trees they had known in their eastern homes—
the maples and the sycamores—but not even careful watering
could help them adapt to the wild extremes of heat and cold or
to the warming Chinooks which fooled them into life months
too early, then froze the sap solid in their trunks. Only the
native cottonwoods seemed able to survive, and settlers brought
them up from the creek bottoms and riverbanks and planted
them around their farmyards. They planted the caragana, too,
an impossibly hardy Asian that would thrive in marginal soil
and live on little water. In the spring it would even offer a
bright show of yellow flowers to break the endless brown
monotony.

Out in the Milk River country, from any rise in the land,
trees can be the only mark of some human habitation, past or
present. Most of the people who first planted them were not
here to see the day when they grew dense enough to break the
wind or tall enough to shade the roof, but their regular rectangles have survived to mark the places where so many small
hopes died.

The plains are dry. Above all else, the plains are dry. This
simple assertion is fundamental to an understanding of the
plains environment, but it is a relative term. That the plains are

flat and largely treeless are facts—obvious, visible absolutes. That they are dry demands comparison. Dry compared to what? To the great rain forests of the Pacific Northwest? To the Sonoran Desert of Arizona and Old Mexico? No. The plains are dry compared to what the first white explorers and settlers had been used to east of the Mississippi. The implications of that relative lack of moisture—a deficiency in some places of perhaps only five or ten percent a year—were not learned easily or quickly, and echoes of the travesties which accompanied the lessons still resonate across the full length and breadth of the high plains.

Not all parts of the plains environment hold the three essential elements in the same combination or exhibit their characteristics to the same degree. The lines which mark the boundaries of the true prairie, delineate the intermountain plateaus or define the limits of the high plains are flexible, and one zone fades unevenly and uncertainly into another. Small changes in elevation or average temperature, even the presence of rivers or the proximity of lakes, can move a line a few miles in any direction or cause it to meander like a pothole creek. On the southern plains of Oklahoma or Texas, absolute rainfall is higher than along the Missouri at the same longitude, but so is the temperature. The net result of higher rain and higher temperature is higher evaporation; what the earth gets to keep is the same, north and south.

Nature does not work with the arrogant, uncompromising certainties of the straight line, but people do. In need of some cartographic consensus, a rallying point to mark where the true prairie meets the high plains, we settled on the 100th meridian as the place where all the rules change. East of the 100th meridian, the true prairie, that small Canadian triangle and the broad, shallow trench of the Mississippi valley (what is today Illinois, Iowa, Indiana, parts of Minnesota, Wisconsin, Ohio, Nebraska and Kansas) is both flat and treeless, but it is not dry. East of the meridian the land lives on between twenty and thirty inches of rainfall per year. West of it, there is half that much.

The true prairies, before they were plowed into oblivion, were tallgrass. In a perfect niche, the pond grasses and the big bluestems could reach ten feet in height, and there are stories of early travelers standing in the stirrups just to get their bearings. On the prairie, with its greater humidity and subsurface moisture, the huge grasses drove their roots deep, aerating the soil and enriching it over the centuries through which it stood undisturbed.

The high plains are home to the shortgrasses, gramas and wheatgrasses which nowhere approach even half the height of the prairie giants. Half the rain equals half the growth, and a shorter growing season dictates that growth be more explosive and less luxuriant. Lower levels of in-ground moisture keep the roots closer to the surface and leave the soils beneath a thin, nutrient-poor hardpan. Everything on the high plains lives closer to the skin, both above and below, and there's no surplus to invest in chance taking.

When the moldboard plow peeled the ten-thousand-year-old sod off the prairie, the amalgam of sufficient moisture, rich soils and brutally efficient agriculture combined to create the best and, for now, most profitable farmland on the continent. This is the Corn Belt and the heart of winter wheat country, the breadbasket of the nation, if not (as they like to say) of the world. When that same plow hit the high plains half a century later, the result was a disaster of incalculable proportion. West of the 100th meridian, nothing was the same.

Today, it's easy to let more than a century of data on rainfall, wind velocity, evaporation and flow rates define the nature of the high plains and ink a clean line around the Great American Desert. Still, for all the accumulated data, the line has not moved far since it was first drawn onto the maps by the earliest white travelers. Today, we may know more, but we do not know different.

Zebulon Pike saw a desert along the Arkansas River as he headed toward the Rockies in 1810. So did Bradbury and Brackenridge, traveling to the north a year later. So did Nuttall in 1819. Stephen Long saw it all around him on the Platte River in 1820 and on his map "Great Desert" is written large and in boldface all the way from the meridian to the mountains.

Canadian-backed explorer Henry Hind first dragged the phrase north of the 49th in 1857 and applied it to the whole of the border country between Manitoba and the Alberta foothills. Photographer Humphrey Hime was with him and brought back the pictures to prove the description was accurate. John Palliser told his British sponsors the same thing at about the same time, and his name has become synonymous with the place: Palliser's Triangle.

Like dry, desert is a relative term. What we take it to be today, a scientific definition alloyed with *National Geographic* images of sand dunes and Tuaregs, is narrower than it was in the nineteenth century. Prone to what now seem excessively poetic turns of phrase, early writers used the word to describe almost any conditions which were less hospitable than those they were accustomed to. Perhaps, too, in their eyes the land seemed deserted. It's hard sometimes to know where scientific objectivity left off and general distaste began.

Stephen Long saw "a dreary plain, wholly unfit for cultivation, and of course uninhabitable by a people depending upon agriculture for their subsistence." "May the place," he intoned, "forever remain the unmolested haunt of the native hunter, the bison and the jackall." Others were even less flattering. Looking south and west toward the Milk River from the more comfortable climes of the Cypress Hills, Palliser saw, stretching away to the horizon, "a region of arid plains, devoid of timber or pasture of good quality," its sage- and cactus-covered soils "baked into a compact mass under the heat of the parching sun." With this duly entered in his journal, he went no farther south.

That there is desert in the West—honest to God sand dune desert—cannot be contested. Hundreds of miles before Death Valley there are fields of shifting sand in western Nebraska which look every inch Saharan. Even southeastern Saskatchewan now boasts of its Great Sand Hills, but such things are extreme anomalies, breaks in the endless grass. The change from true prairie to desert is infinitely more subtle. Too subtle for the first settlers to notice.

The first homesteaders to drift beyond 100° west were not ignorant men. They were not European city dwellers or Maine loggers; they were farmers. They were the sons and daughters of the prosperous Mississippi Valley. The land on which their fathers had cut the deep sod fifty years before was all taken up, and as their fathers had done they sought their own homesteads in the farther West.

South of the border, the idea that the Great Plains were one unbroken, unrelenting wasteland had peaked and begun to decline by the time of the American Civil War. More detailed topographic studies, combined with the reports filtering back from the trappers and those who took the first wagons along the Santa Fe and Oregon trails, showed the plains to be as complex as they were wide. There were upland areas of relief from the dry grasslands, protected places where the rainfall seemed sufficient and river valleys where the water ran steadily all summer. Chinook belts could be counted on to break the hard freeze of the half-year northern winter, and in the south real winter weather was brief and sporadic.

If it was not literally true for the whole compass of the plains, the word *desert* should at least have struck a cautionary note for those who sought to farm it. The problem was that the lands immediately west of the meridian did not look like a desert. As the homesteaders moved deeper into the plains, the grasses still seemed rich enough—barely different from those which had covered the prairies just to the east—and the lack of trees, while a costly impediment to the building of houses and barns, at least meant that the huge job of blowing and pulling stumps would not figure in the creation of farmlands. For those first settlers, it defied logic that lands which had support-ed countless millions of buffalo were incapable of producing crops. Most damaging of all was that the first homesteads west of the meridian were established at the beginning of a cycle of relatively high rainfall, and the first crops were spectacular. As Wallace Stegner wrote:

> Farmers put their foot in the door and waited. When nothing happened, they poked their heads in. When nothing still happened, they went all the way through. What had seemed to Pike a permanent barrier against settlement became a garden, a Canaan.

When the idea of the plains as a wasteland collapsed, it was replaced by a simplicity every bit as dangerous: the plains were Eden itself. Just as early traders and explorers *knew* there had to be a northwest passage because they so desperately needed one, so the early homesteaders *knew* the West was rich because their dreams and their experience told them it had to be. The West would teach them that things are never as simple as they seem.

The roads which border the Milk River country—Alberta 501, Montana 232 and a dozen others even less traveled—are littered with the picturesque wreckage of the grinding collision between booster dreams and hard reality. The weathered shells of slumping houses, shot-sided barns and grain bins are the wistful, *de rigueur* subject for amateur oil paintings and tourist photographs. They also mark the high tide line of homesteading in the Prairie West.

The great triangle which stretched along the border from the 100th meridian to the Alberta foothills—Palliser's Triangle—was the last western place to go under the plow and the first to blow away. In barely two decades after 1909, when the great drylands were opened to settlement, the margins of the Milk River country were divided, fenced, seeded to wheat and blown into oblivion. The rush had peaked by 1919, and by the time the "real" depression began in 1929, the lands between the Sweetgrass and the Cypress Hills already lay in ruins. By the time the large-scale government relief programs came into being, there was almost no one left to take advantage of them.

The question is not why the settlement of the triangle was a failure. The question is why the settlement of the triangle was ever attempted at all. Everything about it was wrong from the start, and once it commenced, every remedy for the immediately apparent problems served only to make matters worse.

Villains are easy to find: the railways with their future profits bound up in the millions of marginal acres which had been their reward for building the National Dream; the real estate agents and chambers of commerce with huge, speculative investments in stores, hotels and lumber yards; the politicians and do-gooders with their visions of a new Eden. They all preyed on the farmers and would-be farmers who flocked to the new lands and jammed the streets in front of the land offices at Lethbridge and Medicine Hat every time new sections were opened, trying to file on land they had probably never seen.

Careful scholars like the University of Calgary's David Jones have collected and studied the individual stories of these people who never really had a chance. That some of them were simply fools, there can be no doubt. Most, however, were not senseless dreamers. They were the sons and daughters of farmers, people who had grown up in rural America and knew how to farm. They knew the land they were settling was dry, drier than the places from which they had come, but they did not understand the implications of that dryness. They had read the booster accounts of spectacular yields (some the truth of the few wet years but most the product of wishful thinking or outright falsehood) and had been born with the Victorian's industrial age instinct for accepting that men of science could solve any problem. If faith, determination and hard work were all it took, the Milk River country would indeed have blossomed like the promotional pamphlets and government propaganda promised.

But all the hard work in the world could not have saved the dryland farmer. Underpinning the sad portraits which Jones presents in his *Empire of Dust* is the single, hard factor which would blunt and defeat determined dreams at every turn: there is simply not enough reliable rainfall to grow wheat or almost anything else in the heart of Palliser's Triangle.

Jones mined government reports and statistical profiles, meteorological data and financial statements, and he lards his text with the reality of life in the drylands. While there had been bumper crops in 1915 and 1916, they were the exceptions which proved the rule. From the opening of the drylands in 1909, the crops had largely failed in 1910, 1914, 1917, 1918 and 1919. In the twenties, impossibly, things got even worse, disaster following disaster, until there was nothing left.

The reason is simple. While the average annual precipitation for the area around Medicine Hat is perhaps twelve or thirteen inches, between 1900 and 1936 it fell below eleven inches fully sixteen times. Even if the rain fell at precisely the right times and in precisely the right amounts (which it almost never did), less than eleven inches is not enough.

Neither government agents nor speculators were entirely ignorant of the particular problems presented by turning the drylands under the plow. Earlier experience along the margins in the Dakotas and Saskatchewan had exposed the need for nurturing what little in-ground moisture there was, and dozens of surefire methodologies had been promoted in newspapers, farm journals and government reports on both sides of the border for thirty years or more before Palliser's Triangle was thrown open. Every method had the ring of truth about it: authorship by a Doctor Someone-or-Other, the imprimatur of a university or government agency or better yet the sworn testimony of actual farmers who had grown rich by following the advice. In the final analysis, though, what made it all so plausible was the same willing suspension of disbelief which had dogged the opening of the West since the time of La Salle: that faith can weave truth out of fantasy.

Some solutions seemed to make sense. Homestead acts on

both sides of the border had been amended to make the basic unit of dryland settlement 320 acres, double the traditional quarter section. This change acknowledged that the summer-fallowing and crop rotation crucial to preserving soil moisture could not support a family on 160 acres. While recognizing that the drylands required different rules was a beginning, in truth, 320 acres were not nearly enough either.

As early as the 1860s, John Wesley Powell, the first great dryland realist, had seen the West for what it was. His 1878 *Report on the Lands of the Arid Region of the United States* was a clear, concise prophesy of what would happen if the farming habits of the East were brought across the 100th meridian. As usual, Powell's truths were recognized only in the perfect vision of hindsight. Not 160 acres, he had said, nor 320, but 2,560: four full sections must be the minimum homestead in the heart of the arid lands. This he said in the full knowledge that such an allotment would be beyond reason for farmer and promoter alike.

The drylands presented a contradiction at every turn. With a year-round creek, 160 irrigated acres might be enough if a homesteader could afford the cost of bringing the water to his fields. Three hundred and twenty acres in a pocket of reliable rainfall would be enough if one unmechanized family could manage that much land.

Four full sections, however, were out of the question for anything but cattle. No turn-of-the-century family farm could operate on such a scale and no townsite-promoting chamber of commerce would put up with it. The implications of such infl-ated homesteads would be a mathematical deathblow to their dreams of development.

Rain follows the plow. Every expert knew that. Plow deep,

they told the homesteaders. Turn the grasslands upside down and the rain will come. And when the rain didn't come, they told them to summer-fallow. Plant one crop in three years or two; give the wheat two years of moisture to make one season of growth. Plow the land deep and keep it clean, free of water-robbing weeds. Trap the moisture in the ground with a mulch of dust and save it up for next year's wheat. There were small pockets where the results were spectacular. There were places where farmers had enough land to allow one half of it to lie fallow. But then the winds began to blow, and the soil and the dust mulch and the hopes for next year's bumper crop darkened the skies a thousand miles away. It was all about applying experience and logic to a land which knew nothing of either. It was all about perfect timing in a place which defied the calendar at every turn.

People who live on the land keep their chronicles by the weather, remembering the passing years like the Blackfeet with their winter counts, reducing twelve long months to the one singular event which marked the year as different from those which came before it. Out in Pendant d'Oreille, north of the Milk River near the broad alkaline flats of Pakowki Lake, the local historians built such a chronicle into the Jubilee history of their place. Year by year, they took the measure of living in a dry land:

1909—open winter, mild, hardly any snow. Settlers began to arrive.

1910—awfully dry. Not even green grass.

1911—good crop year, but not many had fields broken yet.

1912—good crop year.

1913—fair crop year.

1914—very dry. Grasshoppers too.

And on into the twenties:

1919—again very dry and difficult.

1920—a little better, but grasshoppers bad.

1921—a little better. Grasshoppers very bad.

1922—hailed out.

1923—pretty good.

1924—really dry again. Settlers began to leave.

And on it goes, on through the thirties and forties, through the good years of the fifties and the middling sixties. It ends with 1970: "Mild winter, no snow. Dry spring. Rains in June. Crop—?? Wait and see." The words did not change, but through the decades everything else did. The tiny parcels of free land disappeared. Proved up or not, the quarter sections and half sections of homesteader dreams were swallowed up and consolidated into fields of a full section and more. The fantasies of rain and plows, of broad, clean summer fallows and a dozen other surefire remedies were purged by hard pragmatism and the knowledge that the rain would come when it did, if it did, and the best one could do was be ready for it.

The horses were gone, and the huge, plodding steam traction engines soon followed them into history. Faster and more powerful diesels pulling huge gangs of cultivators and seeders could sweep across the massive fields in an almost military exercise of rapid deployment, responding to whatever brief moments of opportunity the weather allowed. In spring, late enough into the fields to catch the weeds, not so late as to lose the early moisture. In autumn, late enough to let the grain mature, not so late as to tempt the first hard freeze or early October blizzard.

That little gray home in the West never really had a chance out here in the Milk River country. All that's left are the faces in the old photographs, squinting into the sun under bonnets and straws, standing resolute before their tiny shacks of warping, rough-sawn clapboards. All that there was of them except their spirit has been buried under the huge, striped blankets of big business wheat, ground into memory under the wheels of the massive tractors.

Along the margins of the endless fields or behind the industrial Quonset huts that pass for barns out here, worn-out plows and seeders gather weeds and rust. In places they have been painted and parked in flower beds between rows of wagon wheels, keeping a nostalgic connection to the old times. But the real symbols of what it took to hold this country stand in the implement dealers' lots beside the highway in Milk River and every other town of any size across the high plains West. Shining in their flagship colors—cherry red for the Case Internationals, green and yellow for the John Deeres and a gaudy, fluorescent lime for the Steigers—this state of the art in farm tractors is by any measure an awesome sight. Massive and boxy, like something a giant child would build with outsized Lego blocks, the beast is nothing more than the sum of its complex systems, a perfect expression of form following function. An articulated mass of gears and hydraulic connections, the tractor is designed to move all day at the same steady crawl, up hill and down, sucking its subsidized diesel at the rate of ten gallons per hour or more. Eight huge wheels shod with herringbone tires sixty inches high lift the floor of the cab and its wraparound tinted glass a full eight feet above the land. All this high-tech power and comfort comes with a price tag that can easily top two hundred thousand dollars.

Produce more wheat! Everything conspires toward this huge singularity, locking the farmer into an endless spiral of growth at any cost. But to grow more wheat, there has to be more land, and the need to summer-fallow means two acres to make one acre of grain. More land means more fertilizers and herbicides and bigger machines to work them in. More wheat means more to plant and more to harvest in the same narrow windows of time. More to harvest means more swathers and combines and eighteen-wheel trucks to haul the wheat away to the distant elevators. More machines means more diesel and tires and over-priced parts and more outbuildings to keep them all in. And the only way to pay for it all? Produce more wheat!

When the pendulum swung across the generations, from grandfather to grandson, it swung with a vengeance, scything everything in its path. Down came the fences, the windbreaks and the old homeplaces, swept away by giant machines. It was as if some new mechanical glacier had come down onto the country, grading the rises into the ponds and leveling out the imperfections to create its own environment, one best suited to its own limitations. Buoyed on a sea of subsidized diesel, tax breaks and guaranteed prices, the grain men pushed and plowed into the hardest margins of an already marginal land. Where cheap water could be engineered into the fields, they pumped it in the millions of gallons, pouring it onto the ancient seabed salts, coaxing the crops to grow in places where Nature said they should not be.

In fairness, we gave them no choice, no other way to stay on their land and do what they had always done. We locked them into that circle of growth and dependence and dependence on growth. We would not let go of our old homestead fantasies, preferring instead to sustain them with proud images of the family farm as the soul of the nation, of free men and women putting the food on our tables and feeding a starving world. It's nice stuff for electioneering, for Canada Day speeches and slick documentaries, but even the most hardened of pork barrel politicians knows it cannot go on any longer.

Unwilling and increasingly unable to feed the farming industry more than it can produce, we are turning our backs on the old vision, finally abandoning our dreams for these places and telling those who would live here that they must begin to do so at their own risk. Sadly, there will be no gentle weaning. When we lose interest in something, even something we have cared for deeply, we drop it quickly and completely like a child suddenly bored by a favorite toy. The freight subsidies are gone, and they will take with them the short line railways and the elevators and what's left of the small towns. The marketing boards will be next to go, along with the stabilized prices and the guaranteed markets.

In the next few years, the modern, mechanized farmer will face the same relentless weeding that decimated his grandfather's horse-drawn, homestead generation. The same rough realities will again begin to grind against the weak and the inefficient. Those with the best land, those who understand what is best for their land, will survive as they did before. They will find new crops and new ways to grow them. And they will send the margins back to grass, the way they should always have stayed.

Out on the huge, open ground, standing in the shadow of the massive machine, I find it hard to reconcile the two images. On one hand, the sepia-toned frame of the homesteader, leaning his back against the reins, hands wrapped tightly around the plow handles; on the other, his grandson, ten feet tall in an air-conditioned greenhouse, effortlessly engraving his perfect geometry across more land in one day than the old man could ever have imagined, seeming to take almost the breadth of the old homestead just to turn the thing around. And yet they are the same people, working the same land against the same odds, vulnerable to the same shifting circumstances which always seem just beyond their control. Only the scale is different. It's just that in Milk River country the scale is everything.

History accretes upon itself, the sun advances several
degrees, and we move farther into the Holocene.
—DON GAYTON

A DESERT
MADE BY
WATER

*T*he plains are flat. The Great Plains have always been
flat. For hundreds of millions of years, they have been
a grand exercise in plane geometry. Even as they floated about the globe, connected to and then detached from one
ancient super-continent or another, subjected to stresses and
strains beyond imagining, they remained flat and unbroken.

Out on the plains in midsummer, there is nothing to offer
shelter from the relentless sun or the constant wind. It has been
weeks since the last rain and the small creeks and pothole
ponds are down to their last trickle of muddy water. As the sun
and the wind dry the beads of sweat of on my face almost
before they have formed, it is hard to accept that this land once
held water in unimaginable abundance, that for millions of
years it was the floor of a succession of inland seas and later
lay frozen under a thousand feet of glacial ice.

With the plains, what you see on the surface is what you
get for thousands of feet below. Exposed by the cutbanks and

coulees, it is layer upon countless layer of smooth sediments in a bewildering variety of color and texture. Water made these rocks, pressing shales and sandstones from the settling dross of a succession of inland seas and river-broken mountains, capped by rough glacial till and outwash. Still, as rocks go, it's all new, barely adolescent stuff. Imagine the earth's history compressed into a single century and nearly ninety years had passed before the making of the plains even began.

Along the Milk in Canada, there is little evidence of the huge subterranean forces so obviously at work in the Rockies only sixty miles to the west. From the east slope foothills through to the Pacific, relief is magnificently positive, a gravity-defying succession of crumpled, foreshortened planes spiked up by continental collisions. On the plains, relief is negative: the slower, steadier work of water and wind.

Reduced to a dangerous simplicity, there are only two forces at work where the plains meet the mountains: orogenies to build mountains and erosion to tear them down. The first is spectacular, accomplished in the blink of a geologic eye. The second is quieter, almost routine. It's the hare and tortoise fable played out on a continental scale, and the result is inevitably the same. In the battle between orogeny and erosion, erosion cannot lose. Gravity cannot lose.

The shape of the southern Alberta Rockies may be different from the plains, but the they are made largely of the same stuff: the limestones, sandstones, shales and silts accumulated over more than six hundred million years of gradual deposition onto the metamorphic and igneous rocks of the Precambrian Shield. The shield itself, the defining surface presence east of the prairies, is almost impossible to find on the plains, buried so deep beneath the sediments as to be beyond knowing. Even in the Rockies, Precambrian time shows itself in only a few places. In the deepest southwestern corner of Alberta, in Waterton and Glacier national parks, some Precambrian sediments have been exposed, as they have in Montana's Little Belt and Highwood mountains near Great Falls, but on the plains such exposures are curiosities, exceptions to the rule.

What broke and crumpled the quiet sediments into the Rocky Mountains was the last great event in the 170 million years of the Mesozoic Era. Somewhere beyond 65 million years ago, a time we know as the end of the Cretaceous Period and the end of the dinosaurs, North America's westward drift picked up speed as the Atlantic Ocean began to open. Moving too fast for the eastbound Pacific plate to subduct smoothly beneath it, the lighter continental block rode roughshod up and over it. The resulting forces held the leading edge, planed it back into the oncoming mass and buckled it like a car hood in a head-on collision. It's called the Laramide Orogeny, or the Laramide Revolution, and its effects are still being felt across the whole length and breadth of western North America.

The Laramide Revolution was not a single event but an ongoing series of action and reaction which has been played out in western North America for three-quarters of a billion years or more. While the full story of what has happened and why will never be known or completely understood, two things in the past fifty years have done much to dissipate the fog and bring what we do know into cleaner focus.

First was the rapid development and general acceptance of the principles of plate tectonics, which has become the common thread—the grand unifying theory—for how the geological world works. It explains how the earth's crust is created and destroyed, how the continents move and what happens when they collide. Unmentioned even in my sixties high school science textbooks, tectonics is a new and powerful player in the study of the planet, binding together, in a tight matrix, innumerable observations and speculations about why things are as they are.

The oil and gas industry has drawn a careful, detailed portrait of the effects of plate tectonics in the Milk River country. In their relentless search to discover new fields and define the limits of those they know, companies have undertaken the kind of all-out detailed seismic studies which academic geologists and geophysicists can only dream about. This combination of plate tectonics and oil fever has redrawn the geological map of the West.

In the mid-1980s, when David Alt and Donald Hyndman set out to update their indispensable fifteen-year-old *Roadside Geology of Montana*, they quickly realized that revision would not work. So much had changed in the intervening years that only a completely new text would do. They expect that another fifteen years will require another ground-up rewrite.

The Laramide Revolution put an end to the succession of inland seas which had regularly split the continent. The whole of North America lifted and tilted down west to east, elevating thousands of feet of seabed sediments and reorganizing the ancient river systems into patterns we would recognize today. As the Rockies came up and the seas drained away, the subtropical swamps and shallow bays, which had laid down the raw materials for coal and oil and nurtured the great dinosaurs, disappeared for the last time. Shadowed from rain by the new mountains, the land cooled, dried out and began to bake under the cloudless sky.

The visible results of the colliding plates curve below the Milk River in a gentle arc from the Canadian Rockies southeastward along the Great Divide, in some places simple and obvious, in others impossibly complex. Directly west of the Milk, the front range and its foothills belt end cleanly, and the transition to the true plains is obvious and palpable. There are no mountains on the Canadian plains east of Pincher Creek.

South of the border, the wreckage is manifest in some places more than four hundred miles east of the Canadian divide, expressing its confused climax in the twisted, plaited ranges and boiling earths of Wyoming. In Montana, isolated strips of mountain rise out of the plains almost to the North Dakota line, sharing a longitude not with Calgary, or even Medicine Hat, but with Regina. Midway from Fort Peck to Havre, between the Missouri and the Milk, the Little Rocky Mountains were named for their snow-capped peaks, which deceived first-time travelers into believing they were days closer to the real thing than they were. The Bulls, the Big and Little Snowys, the Little Belts and the Highwoods stand in sharp relief from the rolling grasslands. Though their individual ages and compositions vary, they are all the products of the same revolution.

There's a problem in describing geologic events like the Laramide Revolution. The principles of geomorphology—the way the land looks—are easy enough to grasp. Chester Beaty, in his engaging study *The Landscapes of Southern Alberta*, reduces it all to an elegant simplicity: "The landscapes of any part of the earth's surface consist of forms made by processes acting on materials through time."

The problem isn't with the processes or the materials. It is with the time. It is time which demands the willing suspension of disbelief. The geological here-and-now, the present tense of rocks, covers the last ten million years and recent means four or five times that. We tend to deal with all this indirectly, to speak in metaphor and analogy and reduce huge numbers to simple digits and decimals. It's inevitable given that these are lengths of time almost beyond our ability to grasp. Knocking off all the zeros seems to help. The distance between 3.3 and 3.2 is slight and manageable, but if the figures are millions of years, that tiny difference contains within it almost ten times the number of years that the glaciers have been gone from the plains.

That so many of the rock strata underlying the prairie grasses are the crushed and broken remains of great mountain ranges is hard to conceive. Standing out on the plains, as I look toward the enormous mass of the Rockies, it takes a huge leap of faith for me to imagine there is more of them lying under-foot than is visible against the horizon. Again, time is the key. While the Rockies were still pushing up through the ancient marine sediments, the creeks and rivers of the northern tier had already commenced the work of tearing them down. Seventy million years ago and more, across the full breadth of the Milk River country, the mountains were being washed away and dumped onto the plains. For a time, the mountains rose faster than erosion could take them down, but eventually, inevitably, the water began to win.

If we cannot comprehend that the Rockies will eventually disappear, can we accept that they are eroding away at the rate of three inches in a thousand years? That they have lost just half a pencil length since Leif Ericson stumbled onto New-foundland? To admit that tiny loss in a thousand years is to accept that two hundred and fifty feet of this rock will disap-pear in a million years and five thousand feet in twenty million. It is more than seventy million years since the Rockies came up.

North of the border, the Continental Divide is guarded by

a succession of front ranges, by the Livingstones, Highwoods and Kananaskis, and by the parallel ridges of the foothills belt. Below the line there are no front ranges and foothills. The Lewis Range holds the Great Divide, and the transition from mountain to prairie is immediate and literally precipitous.

The peaks of the Lewis Range are different in more ways than one. The classic mountain-building scenario manifested west of Calgary—the jagged north–south chains with their crumpled carpet of foothills—does not apply here.

Typically, the collision of moving plates compresses and breaks the sediments, driving the oldest up through the newest, making mountains with ancient cores and younger flanks. For reasons known (or guessed at) only by those who make their lives learning about such things, the slow-motion tectonic crash which fashioned the Continental Divide south of Pincher Creek did not follow the model. Some unique meeting of force and resistance, some particular pattern of flaws or folding, worked to rewrite the relationship of cause and effect in Glacier Park.

It's called an overthrust fault. In Glacier Park country, it's called the Lewis Overthrust Fault, and it was here, at the end of the nineteenth century, that such things were first recognized by geologists. Simply put, the horizontal, *mille-feuille* strata of the peaks are eons older than the rocks on which they rest.

The Lewis Range is ten thousand feet of billion-year-old stones sitting on top of sediments one-tenth or less their age. When the big plates collided, the leading edge of the nearly flat fault ducked into the Precambrian strata, shouldered them up and slid them back toward the east on a shallow incline plane of soft Cretaceous rock. And there they sit now, forty miles or more to the east of where they were first laid down on

the beds of their ancient seas: a fleet of massive galleons driven
hard aground on a packed sand beach.

Alt and Hyndman make it easy to read the hundreds of
millions of years revealed on the bare face of Glacier Park's
mountains: Altyn limestones are the deepest of the Precambrian exposures, a pale tan low on the exposed valley walls, almost
white where the roadcuts are deep and new. Thirty-five hundred feet of green Appekunny mudstones rest on the Altyn,
and above them twenty-five hundred more of Venetian red
Grinnell mudstones, grading out of the Appekunny in alternating layers. Stacked onto this are another thirty-five hundred feet
of gray limestone, divided near the top by a clean, black band
of basalt, a molten volcanic rock squirted into the limestones
after their deposition. The icing on this slab of layer cake is the
bright red Kintla mudstone, capping the highest peaks along
the divide.

The textbook approach to telling what all this stuff is and
how it came to be here makes the facts simple to absorb, but it
cannot help my mind grasp the monumental forces and near-
boundless time it took to make it all so. When I look up from
the guides and step back from trying to identify each of its
particular parts, the sheer, indifferent mass of the front wall
instantly and utterly defeats any attempt to comprehend it.

There is no problem in seeing the geological history of the
Milk River country. It is in evidence everywhere. Everywhere
there is a coulee or gully, hundreds of thousands—even millions—of years of steady change lie exposed to the continuing
work of wind and water. The geologic chart of southeastern
Alberta shows the surface formations as a bewildering series of
concentric circles spreading out from the Cypress and the
Sweetgrass hills, following the valleys of the Milk and the

South Saskatchewan. Between the heights of the Cypress Hills, with their exposures of buff-colored silts and sandstones, and the deepest reaches of the Milk River canyon, lined with the gray shales of ancient salt water beaches, a full twenty million years of accretion and erosion tell the story of the huge yet infinitely subtle forces which have always been at work here.

Armed with Beaty's study, the Alberta geological highway map and the certainty that a little knowledge is a dangerous thing, I floated the middle reaches of the Milk River on a cloudless day in early August. The river was full and steady, flowing dark green over a clear gravel bottom. Nowhere more than two or three feet deep, it broke easily into shallow riffles around the inside of every turn, adding sand and smooth stones to the broad flats that ran back to the edge of the valley. Around the outside of the curve, where the water had to move faster, it pushed hard against steep cliffs, and the sure signs of the unending work of the river were everywhere. Wherever it touched the smooth sandstones supporting the valley walls, the river was steadily eating them away. In places, the river had cut shallow caverns three or four feet back under the face of the cliff, and the wall above already seemed to defy gravity. Though strong and resistant when dry, the wet sandstone seemed to lack any structure at all, and I could claw it out by the handful with little effort. This was all that was holding up the valley wall and I was convinced that next year's spring runoff or next week's sudden, drenching thunderstorm—or even the few handfuls I had dug away—would be enough to bring the whole thing crashing down into the riverbed.

The story of this country stretches away up the sheer cliffs. The smooth bands of pale ochre and soft gray look every bit the beach sand they used to be when the ebb and flow of ancient seas split the continent time and time again. Between the old sand beaches, gray-brown lines mark the strata of silt and mud, caught and pressed to stone when they drifted down into the margins of the huge, shallow seas.

Atop the smooth strata of sand and silt, the wall becomes rougher, less finely lined, and I think I can read the place where the land began to tilt again and the salt water drained away for the last time. The striations are wider and filled with a random pattern of small, smooth stones locked in a matrix of pale, dried mud. The closer the layers are to the top of the cliff, the rougher and less compacted they become, but all are straight and parallel. There is none of the tortured twisting that marks the mountain places where the plates collided.

I can't tell the names of all these bands (my map does not make such fine distinctions), but I might be looking up at the Frenchman Formation or the Ravenscrag, named for the places in Milk River country where they were first identified. Less than sixty-five million years old, this is all newer stuff. Perhaps it's the broken, outwash remains of the Rocky Mountains; maybe it's even fresh enough to be glacial. I don't know exactly, and I tell myself I should take a course in basic geology or at least come back down this river in the company of a geologist.

As the massive power of the continental collision and the pull of ancient rivers built the foundation of this country, so the more recent work of ice defined its surface form. Clear evidence for presence of ice is everywhere in the benchland mesas between the Sweetgrass Hills and the mountains. Kevin, Montana, sits on flat ground in a broad swale, encircled to the north and west by more than a few hundred feet of sheer escarpment. Though this country looks nothing like the softer cuts and valleys which mark the land just a few miles to the east, the face of the escarpment shows the same pattern of hundreds of thin, sedimentary layers marking the long-departed inland seas, the broken remains of the eroding Rocky Mountains and the old glacial meltwater lakes. Below the visible sediments, the cliff meets the valley floor in a steep talus slope which says the deadly combination of erosion and gravity is continuing to work its slow, certain change on the land.

West of Kevin, toward Cut Bank and Glacier Park, Highway 215 comes out of the valley at thirty-five hundred feet and emerges onto another broad plain, more undulating than the one below but still largely flat. With another short climb to another broad plain, the peaks of the divide are suddenly visible clear down to their roots.

The land here does not roll up toward the mountains in a series of steadily elevating parallel ridges the way it does in the foothills west of Calgary. Here, the underlying strata were undisturbed by the upthrusting Rockies, and the roadcuts show little of the folding or faulting evident north of the 49th. What cut the shape into this land was water not tectonics.

In the heart of the northern benchlands, among the flattop mesas and low buttes just west of the town of Cut Bank, the great glaciers of at least two ice ages reached their farthest point southwest, stalled and began to die. Here, two major alpine glaciers spilled out of the Rockies onto the plains and met the leading edge of the great continental ice sheets coming down from central Canada.

The penultimate glaciation, known in Montana as the Bull Lake Glaciation, covered the Milk River country and most of the northern tier between one hundred and thirty and seventy thousand years ago. As they crested and began to recede, meltwaters from the front of the three main glaciers pooled into

Glacial Lake Cut Bank. Evidence of its changing waterline is faintly visible nearly four thousand feet above current sea level. Blocked at its southern end by a series of unstable ice dams, it regularly overflowed into the massive Glacial Lake Great Falls.

When the ice moved in, the main river systems on the northern plains were probably already long established in much the same relationship as they now are: the South Saskatchewan, then the Milk, the Marias and the Missouri. Farther south than that the glaciers did not reach. There is still a good deal of disagreement about what the ice did to the rivers' paths, but there are scars on the lands between the Milk and the Missouri which suggest it had a profound if temporary effect.

Running south from the town of Milk River, across the border and on through Kevin and Shelby, is a broad, shallow trench. It is known accurately if not poetically as the Sweet-grass Sag. Below Shelby, the trench turns east, tracing a line between the Missouri and Highway 2 as far as the present-day community of Big Sandy. From Big Sandy, the Sag runs north and east to meet the Milk River near where it flows into the town of Havre. The trench is interesting because today it carries no stream which could have been capable of cutting it. Its connection to the Milk River, though, suggests that as the ice sheets approached their farthest point south they bulldozed the course of the Milk ahead of them, merging it with the Marias, making one river flowing east toward the glacial Missouri.

The Missouri, too, might well have been pushed south by the glaciers, leaving an ancient route that took it toward Hudson Bay. Speculation has it that before the ice came, the Missouri veered from its present course somewhere between Great Falls and Fort Benton, following a more northerly path, cutting the present-day canyons of the Big Sandy Creek and the lower

Milk between Havre and Fort Peck. Even at the height of the glacial meltdown, neither the Big Sandy nor the Milk could have incised these valleys so wide and deep.

When the ice retreated, so did the Milk and the Marias. The same landforms which had given them their original course were still there, and the two rivers returned naturally to them. The Missouri, however, stayed where it was, where it is today. A stream so much larger than the sum of all the others, it had carved the steep, narrow canyons of the Missouri Breaks and could not wear its way out. In this complex of sags and abandoned trenches, some geologists see only the courses of ancient outflows from the waning glaciers; others see the Missouri, the Marias and the Milk. It's a discussion unlikely to find resolution.

It's tempting to oversimplify the Milk River country, to connect it by grand generalities with the whole of the high plains. The plains are dry land made by water, semidesert cut and shaped by massive rivers which swelled and boiled to impossible size and then suddenly were gone.

But this northern corner of the shortgrass ocean is a place of particulars, a place made unique by ancient forces conspiring here as they did nowhere else on the continent. The work of ice against mountain is profound and obvious. Twisting, preglacial stream beds are ground into broad, U-shaped valleys with huge basin cirques at their heads. Some are flooded by chains of deep, narrow lakes like those at St. Mary and Waterton. Everywhere are rough moraines of unsorted gravel mounded up to mark some change in the direction, speed or shape of the glacier.

Out on the plains, the signature of the ice is harder to read. By the time the glaciers had reached out and down into the

Milk River country, they were thin, slow moving and pushing their limits. Their presence on the land was brief, and the changes they made were more gentle than those they wrought to the north and west. Students of such things know the ice was here only by what it left behind. West of Cut Bank, the retreating Two Medicine and St. Mary glaciers abandoned the boulders they had brought with them from the Rockies, littering the plains with broken Precambrian sediments of gray limestone and red mudstone. To the north and east, the continental sheets left the proof of their great journey in the form of igneous pink granite and gneiss, Precambrian bedrocks bulldozed perhaps all the way from northern Manitoba.

One after another, great glaciers came down in slow procession to cover the Milk River country but went no farther. How many there were and when they came is still uncertain, but the last, so far, was the Laurentian, and the record of its passage is gently written everywhere across the country.

Perhaps fifteen thousand years ago, latitude and a general warming combined to stall the Laurentian's progress and begin to drive it back, but even then its leading edge was already thin and weak. The ice had been flowing inexorably south and west for fifty thousand years, and by the time it came down onto the high plains it was aged and almost benign. Scouring the scarps between the old riverbeds and filling the preglacial valleys with till and sedimentary rubble, the ice leveled the land, smoothing its contours and reducing its relief, but the massive sheet wreaked no havoc as it drifted in and slowed to a halt. Only in its death throes did the great glacier carve a clear and dramatic record of its presence into the Milk River country in the form of the great coulees.

Couler the early French travelers had called them, from their verb "to flow." Meaning to name only the smaller, narrower cuts that eastern visitors still want to call gullies, the French probably would not have included the broad sweeps of Verdigris and Etzikom coulees in their definition. They might have seen water flowing through these valleys, but they could not have known or even imagined how much water there once was nor how quickly the coulees had come into being.

The courses cut by brief, massive rivers still show across the whole of the Milk River country, giving it a shape that is unique on the high plains. With names like Chin and Forty Mile, Kipp, Pakowki and Seven Persons, the great coulees tell the story of how the Milk River country was made. As the glaciers stalled and stagnated and began to die, the melting ice pooled into broad, shallow lakes along the line of retreat, their silt- and clay-choked waters depositing fine, smooth sediments across the flats below the highlands. Such a huge lake lay between Lethbridge and Taber, and another even larger lay north of the Milk River Ridge. Today, the towns of Magrath and Raymond sit on the broad plane of the old lake bed, remarkable, even in this horizontal country, for its lack of relief. Time and again, the lakes grew until they breached their basins and poured out along some line of least resistance, creating huge, temporary rivers which carried the water away toward the Milk and the Missouri. As the lakes drained and the power of the waters ebbed, the rocks and silts they carried would drop and build new dams and the lakes would grow again in some new configuration. And they would breach again, and build again until the glacier was gone. This was not the slow, inevitable work of mountain water against rock. Current thinking has each of the big coulees made in an instant, cut to its current shape in a matter of weeks, perhaps even days, by the collapsing of the unstable dams and the grinding power of the massive runoff.

The glaciers went back the way they had come, retreating to the northeast or shrinking back into their mountain valleys. Their combined meltwater, still blocked by ice to the north and west, cut its way south, broke through the Milk River Ridge at Whiskey Gap and Lonely Valley and flooded into the Milk River. As the ice continued its retreat, the hemorrhage grew, cutting the great coulees in succession, west to east.

The water did not want to go this way. Then as now, the plains tilted down toward the northeast, but the ice still conspired with the Cypress Hills to block that natural route and the water went south. Where the ground was soft and even, or the flow of the water powerful enough, the relaxed S-bends of the coulees ran wide and shallow. Where the surrounding rock was harder and more resistant, the water cut narrow, jagged wounds deep into the Cretaceous sediments. However it came, smoothly down great spillways or raging through thin, serpentine canyons, the full weight of the melting glaciers continued to pour into the gorge of the Milk River.

About twelve thousand years ago, the size and strength of the Milk peaked and quickly declined. Between the river and the Cypress Hills, in the basin which now surrounds the remnant Pakowki Lake, three great coulees—Etzikom and Chin coming in from the west and Forty Mile from the north—merged and sent their water south through the short chute of Pendant d'Oreille Coulee. Then, as if a wide-open faucet had suddenly been turned off, the water was gone.

When the sheets of ice broke their connection to the Cypress Hills, the fundamental preglacial shape of the land reasserted itself, U-turning the meltwaters away from Pakowki

Lake and up through Seven Persons Coulee, skirting the northern flank of the hills and cutting (or perhaps recutting) the course of the South Saskatchewan due east. To the west, in the shadow of the Rockies, the Milk River Ridge and Hudson Bay Divide proved high enough and strong enough to manage the declining waters, and the Milk was once again the loser. Having carved a canyon fully four hundred feet deep and in places nearly half a mile across, the great river dried up, replaced by something more akin to the thin stream which meanders today across its broad, alluvial bottomland.

From high on the northern shoulder of the Sweetgrass Hills, the great coulees are visible as wide swaths angling across the undulating plain. Most are dry now, their grass-covered sides and bottoms crossed by fence lines and given to the grazing of cattle or the growing of winterfeed. North of the Milk, many of the larger coulees have been dammed and their reservoirs connected to the five-thousand-mile network of irrigation canals lacing the South Saskatchewan basin. Pakowki Lake—"Bad Water" to the Blackfeet—shows much bigger on the maps than it has been for many, many years. Broad, shallow and strongly alkaline, the lake collects a meager runoff from Etzikom and the rest, but today it has no outlet and survives as a huge evaporator, a shimmering, undrinkable oasis in the heart of this dry country.

There once were men capable of inhabiting a river without disrupting the harmony of its life.

—ALDO LEOPOLD

IF THERE
WERE
WATER

At Del Bonita, Alberta Highway 62 becomes Montana 213, its rough two-lane pavement running the thirty-five miles southeast to Cut Bank and Highway 2, known across the breadth of Montana as the Hi-Line. The northern and southern forks of the Milk River, still twenty miles apart, bisect the 49th parallel at the same forty-five-degree angle with Del Bonita exactly halfway between them.

I cross the border onto Blackfeet land just before noon on the last day of summer with a brilliant sun already building a shimmer off the asphalt. There was a hard frost the previous night, but by midafternoon it will be pushing 80° F. A gravel road leading to the west from Montana 213 just a mile below Del Bonita takes me into country I have never seen before. At the intersection, a large plywood sign lists the ranchers and farmers who live here, but the paint is too faded to read any but a few of the dozen or so names. Under the pale blue sky, the land falls away to the south and east. To the west it rises slowly toward the Lewis Range, an irregular, tilted platform etched by the pale gold stubble and midbrown stripes of the huge wheat fields.

The side road west of Highway 213 proves much rougher than it first appears, and where the gravel has been pushed aside, it is a teeth-chattering washboard of packed earth. There are no fences or ditches to divide the fields from the road or from one another; there are no trees and no sagebrush. Nowhere is there a patch of earth that isn't under cultivation. A few horned larks still spin up and away from the side of the road. First to arrive in the spring, they will be the last to leave. Only the occasional solitary hawk still soars over land where just a month ago there would have been a dozen or more to the mile. Probably young-of-the-year wanderers, they may already be well south of where they were fledged.

The harvest is over for this year. The wheat has been cut, combined and stored in the clusters of circular, cone-topped bins along the road or already trucked away south to the elevators along the Hi-Line. Giant eight-wheel tractors, combine harvesters and hauling trucks still stand out in some of the section-sized fields. With no familiar reference to give them scale, the eye reduces the great machines to the size of children's toys.

The gravel twists through the low hillocks and shallow coulees, slowly gaining altitude toward the mountains. On a short straight-away, the only sign for miles, a pellet-riddled black-on-orange square, says simply HILL. A few yards on, and what seemed just another climb over another low rise turns into a quick, steep descent into a broad valley. The view from the rim of the bench is stunning. The peaks of the Rocky Mountain front are a dark, hazy violet and seem from this perspective a two-dimensional cutout pasted onto the horizon. Stretching toward them, the precise strips of wheat stubble and fallow begin to give way to rectangular patches of pale tan shortgrass while, across it all, the sun reproduces in moving shadows the pattern of the broken white clouds.

At the base of the bench, the road and the good gravel both end at a T-junction. To the south it turns into a bare hardpan of packed, black earth. The ruts are clear warning that this road is best traveled only in dry weather or in winter, when it is frozen solid. The road rises steadily up a smooth, rounded hill and silhouetted on the crest is the perfect image. As if conjured by a cinematographer, ten cowboys slowly move a long string of perhaps a hundred Black Angus cattle toward the west. The last of the riders looks briefly toward the sound of the truck climbing the grade, answers my wave and turns back to his work. Under the big hat is a small boy, perhaps ten years old, and through my binoculars the distant look-alike cowboys turn into a whole family: boys and girls, women and men. Any nostalgic notions about the passing of the real West shatter against the fact that this is a life still being lived much as it has been since the first cattle came up into this country.

The next ten miles of winding hardpan are remarkable only for their emptiness, for the complete absence of ranch houses, cowboys, cattle and even birds, and I find myself looking nervously toward the mountains for any sign of coming rain or even a hint of dark clouds. The roads in here, they say, are paved with dehydrated mud, and it would be a long, lonely walk to find a tractor and someone willing to pull my small truck out of the instant, hub-deep quagmire.

Perhaps fifteen miles below the T-junction, the Milk River wanders its way northeast across the floor of a shallow valley. Here, the South Fork meanders up from its birthplace in the shadow of the Lewis Range and picks up the waters of the Dry and the Middle Forks flowing in almost due east from the St. Mary Ridge. This is where the main stem of the Milk River forms.

The precise point of their meeting is lost just above the bridge in a broad swale of dense grasses, reeds and willow thickets, all still a dark, rich green before their first serious freezing. Wherever there is water on this high, dry plateau, the greens can hold on longer. Up the valley sides and along the rim, the shortgrass has already died to dull ochre, but in the bottomlands, a wash of pale olive still fades back from the banks of the river almost to the edge of the slopes.

This beautiful, soft valley holds at its heart the abandoned homeplace of the Consolidated Cattle Company. The low ranch house and bunkhouses, the stables and equipment sheds still stand, surrounded by the corrals and holding pens. The red-stained buildings have yet to begin their slow collapse in on themselves, and only the broken-out white window frames and open doors say that the place is no longer lived in. Pastures and hay meadows stretch far up the valley bottom, giving it its late season tint of green. A newer steel shed and a few pieces of equipment with fresh paint suggest that one of the neighboring ranchers now manages the river valley. Such rare, sheltering land with permanent water and winterfeed is far too valuable to be left fallow.

At work again, the cinematographer summons up a golden eagle flying low and slow across the valley pastures, elevating the picture from the ridge above the ranch into tourist-poster perfection.

Back at the T-junction, another faded sign points north toward the Weathered and Dresen ranches. The Dresen, it says, is 3.2 miles up the road, and I find such a precise measurement odd in this vast, open country. I know how far I have come from Del Bonita, and 3.2 miles would put the Dresen hard up against the border.

North from the junction, the gravel winds down into the valley of the North Milk River. Unlike the southern branch, the valley here is narrow and twisting, its steep sides fluted by ancient runoffs and the almost constant wind. The river meanders sharply through the sand and mud flats of the valley floor, undercutting its banks to expose webs of matted willow roots.

The road crosses the river on a slope-sided concrete slab enclosing three steel culverts. Where the river meets the road, it is perhaps fifteen feet wide and no more than two feet deep, a smooth, green flow over a bed of algae-covered stones in a matrix of dark mud. Even as the day heats up, the steady breeze blowing up the valley and the shadow of the surrounding hills make it a cool, almost pretty place.

Where it runs through the culverts, the North Milk is only four straight-line miles from Canada and barely more than three times that number from its source over near the St. Mary Ridge. The road rises sharply out of the valley and disappears quickly around a curve, turning to meet the border at an unmarked crossing and connect with the Alberta backroad coming south from Taylorville.

A scant mile before it reaches the boundary line, the road will cross another watercourse almost as wide as the North and the South Milk rivers and considerably deeper. Unmarked by any sign or commemoration and barely accessible along most of its thirty miles, the quiet man-made stream between the North Milk and the 49th parallel is a thing of considerable consequence. This slow-moving canal brings the clear, glacial waters the St. Mary into the North Milk and the Missouri River basin.

Dreams of watering the crops of eastern Montana with Rocky Mountain water are as old as the first settlements along the lower Milk. But as a pure plains river, the Milk was utterly incompatible with booster visions of an agricultural Eden along its banks because it would often deliver its spring runoff in one great flood, only to run dry by midsummer. The small irrigation ditches and impounds of the 1880s had taxed the natural capacity of the lower Milk to its limit well before all the available lands had even been sold to the unsuspecting. The Missouri was big enough to provide all the water that settlement could use, but it was far to the south and trapped in the deep canyons of the Breaks, more of an engineering challenge than anyone was prepared to tackle. With no other likely source to hand, the dreamers looked upstream to the headwaters of their own river and saw the solution to their woes tantalizingly close across a single ridge in the cold, deep waters of the St. Mary Lakes. No matter that the St. Mary River flowed north into Canada. No matter that the Milk, too, was at least in part a Canadian river.

The eastern Montanans' need for reliable water and how they proposed to acquire it triggered a high-stakes, bilateral poker game, rife with a sequence of raises, bluffs and calls. In the early 1890s, surveyors from the U.S. Department of Agriculture responded to political pressure from the settlers of eastern Montana by concluding that the only practical solution to their dryland problems lay in a massive transfer of water from the St. Mary to the Milk. They had eyes to bend the whole mountain river to the east. Not only would a diversion be possible from an engineering and a financial perspective, they declared, it also would be perfectly legal. With the point of transfer entirely within the United States, it was none of Canada's business. Besides that, Canada wasn't using the water anyway.

That last rationalization was a test of how far the truth could be stretched. South of Lethbridge, communities of transplanted Mormons were already well advanced on their canals and other reclamation projects. The government formally backed their efforts through the North-West Irrigation Act of 1894, and Canadian officials put their faith in the concept of prior claim and thought little more about it. It occurred to few Ottawa politicians and mandarins that the parched Montanans might not give a tinker's damn for such fine sentiments, especially when there was no law or international agreement to support them. Pushing ahead with its prior claim argument, Canada authorized surveys for an irrigation canal leading from the St. Mary onto the plains north of the Milk River Ridge. The canal, it was believed, would so strengthen the Canadian case for its rights to the water that the Americans would be forced to look elsewhere. It didn't and they weren't.

One year after the Alberta canal's completion, America's Reclamation Act of 1902 brought the proposed diversion of the St. Mary not only the official sanction of Washington at the highest levels, but the likelihood of federal money with which to build it. There would be no water left in the river north of the 49th parallel. The poker game had suddenly become serious.

Canada's first raise had not impressed the anyone. Attempting to intimidate President Teddy Roosevelt, who had made the diversion one of his pet projects, was probably a waste of time. Vested rights and prior claims didn't mean a thing to the Americans (neither in law should it have), and in 1903 they raised back, authorizing the formal survey of the diversion of St. Mary River water. Lacking the cards to raise again and realizing their only hope for saving the St. Mary River lay in an international treaty, the Canadians bluffed. This time, the Americans blinked.

If prior claim meant nothing to the Americans, then there was nothing to prevent Canada from responding in kind. A new canal was designed to take all the diverted water from the Milk River and put it back into the St. Mary where it belonged. In a nice mix of truth and humor, it is known locally as the Spite Ditch. The remnants of the Canadian bluff can still be made out, if just barely, a few yards from where Highway 4 enters the town of Milk River. Though slumped and sagging now, the regular, man-made line of a narrow embankment runs north across the face of the low hills and turns west along the base of the Milk River Ridge.

The higher elevation of the Milk River made a gravity-feed canal back to the St. Mary possible. That the St. Mary basin was only thirty miles away around the Ridge made it practical, and in early 1903 the entire length of the canal was surveyed and staked. Through that spring and summer, the Utah-based Cazier Brothers' construction company managed to build the first fifteen miles, and in the low-water winter of 1903–04 they installed a rock dam across the river a few miles upstream from the townsite.

In November 1904, when the lower portion of the canal—thirty feet wide at its bottom and seven feet deep—was filled with water for the first and only time, it drew the attention of no less a personage than America's Secretary of State. In strong language for a diplomat, John Hay declared that building the canal was an act "lacking in friendlyness." He called for formal talks between the two countries, suggesting at the same time that should an amicable settlement not be reached the United States would investigate other ways to get the St. Mary's water to the lower Milk.

The two countries met the following year and reached an agreement of sorts on the division of the two rivers. Still, no formal resolution was forthcoming for another two years as the Americans continued to look for some way to avoid the Canadian section of the Milk. Though they scoured the lands from the border to the source of the Marias, searching for an easy connection, they found no practical alternative.

Had the Americans looked north toward the Spite Ditch, they might have realized they didn't need one. Whether the Canadian government had dug its canal as a knowing bluff or was serious in the belief that it would preserve the St. Mary for Canadian use is a matter for speculation, but the simple fact is the canal would never have worked. The hills around the base of the Milk River Ridge are almost pure gravel, wonderful for concrete and road building but deadly for a canal. With seepage rates approaching one hundred percent in some places, the canal builders could not keep water in the sections they had completed, let alone across the planned thirty miles back to the St. Mary basin. It was bad surveying and bad engineering, but it was very good politics, and on January 11, 1909, the first boundary waters treaty between the United States and Canada became a reality. To this day, the regulations which it set out still govern the use of the St. Mary and Milk rivers. Canada was guaranteed seventy-five percent of the water from the St. Mary; America got seventy-five percent of the Milk. The U.S. was then free to divert its share of the St. Mary into the Milk according to the original plan.

High above Babb, Montana, in Glacier National Park, meltwaters from the Gem, the Grinnell and the Swiftcurrent Glaciers pour down through a series of lakes and creeks into the head of Lake Sherburne near the Many Glaciers Hotel. They are the first links in a chain of streams, natural and man-made, which carry the American share of waters of the St. Mary River more than three hundred miles east to Havre and the farms of the lower Milk River country.

From the U.S. Department of Reclamation dam across the lake's outlet, Swiftcurrent Creek makes a short, torrential, boulder-strewn run alongside Glacier Route 3 and enters Lower St. Mary Lake almost at the point where the St. Mary River begins its run north toward Alberta. A series of gauging stations between the glaciers and the beginning of the river keep constant track of flow rates and water levels. At a set of head gates less than a mile downstream from where the river begins, a modest canal emerges from its western bank and angles across the valley floor to follow Highway 89 north. The canal parallels the highway for a mile or two, then turns east back toward the river.

Just before the border crossing at the Port of Piegan, an unnumbered gravel road runs east from Highway 89. Less than a mile in, it makes a sharp left-hand curve around the base of a hill and picks up the canal as it makes its way northeast. In tandem, they snake their way along the fluted hillsides. The canal is a cool, dark green, eight feet deep and perhaps thirty feet wide, the lines of its even, regular banks softened by an overgrowth of thick, rich grasses. The flow of the water is barely perceptible.

The road makes a sharp right turn and begins to drop steeply; the canal narrows and disappears into a concrete culvert. At the point where the road crosses the culvert, the land ends abruptly on the rim of the broad valley of the St. Mary River. It is ten miles from the head gates, and the canal has lost only a few feet of elevation, just enough to keep the water moving toward the culvert. The St. Mary is now far below it.

Narrowed and focused through the concrete, the water emerges with a low roar on the other side of the road in two parallel tubes of riveted steel plate. Each more than six feet in diameter, the pipes pitch off the steep drop into the valley and, carried on a wooden bridge, sweep across the St. Mary River, up the low rise on the other side and down into Spider Coulee. Against the soft, rounded hill country, this inverted siphon is a sight as surprising as it is impressive, a deceptively simple and elegant engineering solution to moving water across the Hudson Bay Divide without benefit of pumps or electric power.

Over the ridge in Spider Coulee, the siphon discharges into another slow canal, passes through Spider Lake and wanders east, following the contours of the hills. At Spider Lake, a small sign beside the rough track warns against unauthorized entry, and from this point on, the canal passes only a few ranch compounds, all but one or two of them deserted. After twenty miles and another trip through another inverted siphon, the canal quietly discharges one quarter of the flow of the St. Mary into the North Milk River.

In the first years of the new century, with the firm promise of St. Mary water underwriting the creation of an irrigation district below Havre, the pressures for subdivision pushed in on the lower Milk. Teddy Roosevelt, demonstrating that at least in some ways he understood the natural limitations on western development, created a buffer between the irrigable lands along the Milk River and the dry uplands. This zone, one township wide, was intended to allow the bottomland farmers to summer pasture their cattle while they grew sufficient feed on their irrigated land to carry them through the winter. It was a practical idea that would later take hold on both sides of the border in the driest years of the twenties and thirties, but it was no match for the short-sighted boosterism of the early homesteaders. When Taft replaced Roosevelt in the White House, the buffer zone was thrown open to subdivision.

Land values skyrocketed when the country was opened, and many of the early settlers along the bottomlands sold out and moved on. Prices in the buffer zone soared, too, pushing it out of reach for the cattlemen, who could make the only sensible use of it. Their response was to buy as much irrigated land as possible and keep it in hay, leaving the overpriced uplands to the new settlers. Everything was turned on its head: good, irrigated land which could support mixed farming was growing cattle feed while homesteaders went broke trying to force good, dry grassland to produce wheat. In the succession of drought years which brought the twenties to a close, the wisdom of the buffer became obvious even to the most hardened optimist.

In 1930, what became known as the Malta Plan (named for the river town halfway between Havre and Fort Peck) sought to bring some semblance of reason back to land use practice. Large landowners along the river would agree to sell or lease small parcels to dryland settlers. In return, those drylanders would lease their worthless wheat fields to the cattlemen. All the project needed to make it work was money. The drylanders had little or none, and any they gained from the land swap would be swallowed up by the taxes already owed to the hardpressed governments of Blaine, Phillips and Valley counties. It took Franklin Roosevelt's intervention, in the form of federal relief funneled through the Department of Agriculture, to bring the plan to life.

The project succeeded in bringing relief to the small, mixed farms of the Milk River country and in removing tens of thousands of acres of marginal land from further abuse, but it was a short-term solution. The future of this land was never meant to be built on one hundred and sixty acres, or even on ten times that much.

The Milk River, swelled by St. Mary water, flows free across the breadth of Alberta before turning back across the border just west of the crossing at Wild Horse. Halfway along its fifty mile run from the border down to Havre, the river slows and begins to widen behind the one-hundred-foot wall of the Fresno Dam. The Fresno and its reservoir have been here since 1939, the second stage of the federally financed effort to bring more water more predictably to the lands along the lower Milk.

A low-slung affair of packed earth and boulders which blocks the river at a narrowing in its shallow canyon, the Fresno is the only dam on the Milk River. The graveled county road that runs across the Fresno and over the silver-painted spillway bridge connects U.S. 232 with the Hi-Line, and the views from the top of the dam offer the night-and-day contrasts typical of prairie reservoirs. Upstream, the reservoir is an inanimate pool between the sloping sides of the old river valley. The constantly changing level of the water has left a succession of thin ridges around the base of the hills, like rings around a bathtub. Nowhere is there any sign of the rich greens that water should bring to a dry country. The raw, barren gravels of the reservoir banks give the place a bleak and lifeless look. The small picnic area and boat launch ramp are unused, overgrown and slumping down the edge of the bank at the western end of the dam. It reflects perfectly the whole tenor of the place.

Downstream, I find there is still at least the sense that this is a living river. Fed a carefully monitored flow through the penstock beside the spillway, the river meanders away through the grassy hills toward Havre. The small cottonwoods and clumps of willow along its banks hold swarms of migrating songbirds, all but the yellow warblers showing the standard, frustrating fall mix of dark olive above and buff white below. The narrow mud flats below the dam are still sodden, an indication that the gates have only recently been closed to begin refilling the reservoir. A pair of sandpipers flickers across the flats, looking for anything which might have been exposed by the falling water. In the shallows, the furrowed tracks of large freshwater clams are clearly visible as they respond to the changing depth of the river, making their way down into deeper water. Their empty shells and the hollow remains of crayfish litter the stones above the mud line.

The bodies of a whitefish and a small pike are beached below the dam, and snarls of monofilament fishing line seem to be everywhere underfoot. Along with the pike and the whitefish, the Milk supports populations of sauger, a small, brown variation of the walleye, but it does not hold trout. Recreational boating and fishing are two of the benefits always touted when the rivers of the West are dammed, but the Fresno was constructed before such rationalizations were either fashionable or necessary (and at a time when the natural rivers themselves still held enough fish for anglers).

The Fresno is first and foremost an irrigator's dam, built to store the Milk's brief spring runoffs and the steadier, more predictable contribution of the St. Mary. The dam discharges water into the lower reaches of the Milk to supplement the inadequate and uncertain rainfall. In addition to measuring out irrigation water for the lower Milk, the Fresno Dam is the source of residential water for the eight hundred families living west along the Hi-Line in the small elevator communities of Kremlin, Gildford, Hingham and Rudyard. Havre draws its share directly from the Milk ten miles below the dam. The division of the water has always been a thorny issue, complicated by the obvious fact that both agricultural and residential users are utterly dependent on the croplands for their livelihood.

There are times when the Fresno cannot satisfy both. So great were the irrigation drawdowns in the brutally dry summer of 1988 that they exposed the pumps of the Hill County water system in the middle of the reservoir. The solution of installing new pumps on the downstream face of the dam was coupled with the assurance that there would always be enough water released to keep them primed. That seems to have solved the immediate problem, but it won't last.

The villains are not the residential water users. Their numbers will continue to shrink as Hill and the other border counties slowly but steadily lose population. The small towns are aging, inhabited largely by retired farmers and the few people needed to operate the elevators. If their children do not take over the farm, they do not stay. There is nothing else for them to do. Larger centers like Havre are holding their people, but they are unlikely to grow.

The problem does not lie with the irrigators either, though the long-term damage associated with the protracted dumping of water onto ancient salt seabeds will eventually catch up to them. They do not have the money to expand their operations, and government-funded irrigation projects have become the kind of political dynamite that no one wants to be anywhere near.

The real villain is the very nature of plains rivers, and the Fresno faces the same long-term fate as every other dam on the Great Plains. Sooner or later, some faster than others, they will all be clogged with silt. For older, smaller structures like the Fresno, the problem is becoming serious. Western rivers, by the nature of the lands through which they flow, have always carried large volumes of silt swept into them from the surrounding countryside or from their sources in the constantly eroding mountains. Precipitous rises triggered by brief, brutal thunderstorms or spectacular spring runoffs eat away at their banks of sandstone and compressed gravel, undercutting and dumping their cover of topsoil and tussocks of grass into the stream. Lewis and Clark named the Milk not for its water but for the loads of silt it carried.

Where plains rivers flow unimpeded, their natural dynamics variously pick up and deposit the silts and sediments along their changing course, building new flats one year and washing them away the next. Dams kill rivers, slowing and straightening them, robbing them of the strength to hold and move their cargoes of grit and mud. Behind a dam, the water stalls and the sediments fall out, covering the bottom with a thick mat of ooze that deepens year by year. Nature constructed the plains in the same way, building thousands of feet of sandstone and shale with the slow drifting down of water-borne sediments. But it took Nature hundreds of thousands of years to accomplish what dams do in decades. Over time, the capacity of the reservoir declines, the shallower, turbid water warms and loses its ability to hold oxygen. The thick muds bury the old gravel bottom in a nutrient-free blanket, and the whole system begins to die. Eventually, the dam will neither deliver the volumes of water it was designed to provide nor support the recreation which was supposed to be its value-added benefit.

Even below the dam, where the river might still look healthy and wild, the Fresno will take its toll. Flood control was a promised return for investing in a dam, but floods are far from a destructive force in rivers. They are a danger only to things man-made.

Between them, the Spider Coulee siphon and the Fresno dam have changed the natural rhythm of the Milk River, turning its seasonal variations upside down. The dam contains the heavy spring runoffs, releasing them in the dry of summer when flows should normally be at their lowest. Above the dam, the siphon keeps the water higher and stronger than it should be, eroding the soil and sandstones along its banks, carrying more and more silt down into the Fresno reservoir. Without the water coming in through the siphon over the Hudson Bay Divide, the Milk would barely exist at all, a borderline river in every sense of the word. The net effect is a river bigger than it ought to be, a stream that moves at nearly the same steady rate from breakup to freeze-up, a regulated, unnatural thing that is more canal than living river.

Despite the fact that dams kill rivers, there are people in Alberta who muse about the need for a dam on the upper Milk. In Montana, there are faint hopes for a new dam to replace the aging and steadily silting Fresno, but ideas on where that dam might be are fainter still, and the talk lacks the passion which would have driven it in the fifties and sixties. Among those few who seem to have given the matter serious thought, the consensus is for north of the line, somewhere in the great canyon between the Pinhorn and the border. Reasons why this will never occur go far beyond practicalities, international cooperation and local interest. But even if there were there no problems, where would the water come from? In the dry months, in the dry years, the St. Mary and the Milk are one stream not only by legal dictate, but by fact. More irrigation water for the Milk River country means more water from the St. Mary, and that is unlikely.

There may still be the pervading, unconscious sense that somehow dams make water, that the simple act of piling earth and rocks across a canyon will manufacture more of that priceless commodity. To mention the idea out loud is to make it ridiculous and brook laughing denials, but what else could make otherwise coldly sensible people believe there is vastly more water here than their own eyes tell them? Still, this is the heart of the western drylands, a place where homesteaders were once sold their small parcels on the guarantee that rain would follow the plow, that the simple act of turning the prairie upside down would bring all the water anyone could need.

If it is not foolishness, then something else still fuels the dreams of more water for the fields of the Milk River country. North of the line, the fault may lie in the illusion of plenty that the siphon has created. Above the border, the North Milk is a surprise to any outsider who comes across it. In the small provincial campground just north of Del Bonita, even in a dry summer, the Milk River's banks are a deep green riot of thick grass and cattails. Even as the grasses on the hillsides cure and pale to ochre and the pavement on the highway bridge shimmers and softens in the hot sun, the cliff swallows and red-winged blackbirds circle in their hundreds above the broad course of the river. Since 1917, the North Milk has been this picture of almost wretched excess and it must have been hard, over the years, for farmers who watched their fields dying under a cloudless sky to remind themselves that nearly every drop of this water was already spoken for, that before it even left Montana, the treaty had it measured and marked for Havre and Malta and other places hundreds of miles to the east. St. Mary's glacial water has been flowing through here for so long now that any sense of what the real river was like—of what the real river *ought* to be like—has long since been eradicated from this valley and from the collective memory of those who live along it.

The things which I have seen I now can see no more.
—WILLIAM WORDSWORTH

LIVES
WRITTEN
IN THE SAND

T he Hoodoo Trail snakes east along the Milk River from the campground at Writing-On-Stone Provincial Park. Past the administration buildings, away from the playground equipment and the family campsites, the pathway follows the river upstream along the face of steep, wind-eroded sandstone cliffs. The bright spring greens of the riverbank grass and the silver-blue of the sage bushes surround thick patches of chokecherry and golden currant. Across the river, the darker greens of willow and cottonwood mark the place where Police Coulee cuts up from Montana to meet the river. The distant shouts of the children in the playground come and go against the uncertain swirling of the wind, and the scolding chatter of the cactus wrens up in the hoodoos is the only constant sound. This cool oasis still draws and holds people as it has for thousands of years.

At the end of the trail, across a strong fence, lies the reason that the campgrounds and administration buildings are located at this particular place along the Milk River Valley. On the other side of the fence, scraped and scratched into the sheltering sandstone walls, lies greatest concentration of pre- and post-contact petroglyphs to be found anywhere on the northern plains.

Since 1977, most of the petroglyphs have been separated from the park's campgrounds in an archeological preserve. It is accessible only on daily guided tours in the company of an interpreter. The reason is obvious. Everywhere in the hoodoos which line the edge of the valley floor near the campground, modern visitors have emulated the earliest inhabitants of the plains and have left their names, dates and short messages to posterity. The name of the park is almost an invitation. It's a ritual which white visitors to the site have performed almost from the beginning of their presence in this country, and in the less-visible places east along the riverbank, I find the names or monograms of the turn-of-the-century fence riders and Mounties who were by then the valley's sole inhabitants.

Writing-On-Stone is the single grand exception to the rule about the search for the archeological record of the Milk River country. Away from this place, most of what we have found of the first human inhabitants has been sporadic and, when it comes to prehistory, inconclusive because the nature of the plains environment works against certainties. Few artifacts have survived the flash floods of spring, the scouring winds of summer and the rapid freeze–thaw cycle of Chinook winters. Besides the sandstone drawings at Writing-On-Stone, there are spear and arrow points, teepee rings and not much else.

The drawings at Writing-On-Stone have been known to white history since they were first reported by American James Doty. Secretary, personal assistant and general dog's body to

Isaac Stevens on his treaty-making expedition to the Blackfeet and other upper Missouri and intermountain tribes, Doty crossed the Milk River here in September 1855 on his way north to contact any bands hunting or trading in American territory. Doty's journal records in some detail his encounter with the writings, including a rather odd account:

> In five more miles we struck Milk River at a place called "The Writings", which I had often heard spoken of by the Indians as a locality where white men had many years ago written upon the rocks, and I determined to avail myself of this opportunity to examine into the matter carefully.

Traveling in the company of the Piegan chief Little Dog and comfortable with the Blackfeet tongues, Doty is unlikely to have mistranslated the assertion that the writings were the work of white men, but he seems to have taken the news quite matter of factly.

Such would not have been the reaction in the time of Lewis and Clark. Fewer than seventy-five years before Doty heard there had been white men on the Milk River, there would still have been a fading hope among many Americans and Britons alike that the voyages of discovery up the Missouri would lead to confirmation of one of the West's most enduring rumors: that there was an ancient tribe of "white Indians" living in the heart of the continent. Yet another of the many lost tribe legends (biblical, Chinese, Viking and others) which have long found fertile ground in the Americas, these white Indians were held to be the survivors of a colony of Welshmen founded by their Prince Madoc following his discovery of the New World in 1170.

As the wonderful legend grew and died time and again,

each flowering more lunatic than the last, the Welsh Indians were credited with everything from the Mississippi Valley mounds to the creation of both Mayan and Aztec civilizations. That nearly all of North America had been at least visited by whites by the close of the eighteenth century and that none of them had claimed an encounter with the lost Welshmen made the legend harder and harder to believe. Loathe to let go, one last careful study of the evidence by its die-hard supporters led to the upper Missouri as the certain site of their fabulous villages. The Mandan, it had been widely reported, were light-skinned, red-haired and a spoke language which sounded as much Welsh as anything else. And the upper Missouri was the last unknown, the last place that could harbor wild speculation.

Eventually, like the cities of gold, the inland seas and the Northwest Passage, the Welsh Indians faded into obscurity. As to whether Doty had even heard of the legend, he gives no indication: "Were there ever upon these rocks writings done by the hands of white men, time has long since obliterated them," he concluded.

Any reading of native history of the northern plains quickly dissolves into a confusion of nomenclature. Each of the dozen or so Indian nations which lived in or passed through these lands was known by a host of different names that, along with the infinite variety of spellings provided by early chroniclers, can make a quicksand of the historical record. Names for most of the Indians were coined from some rough translation of what the nations called themselves, what they were called by others, where they lived or what they did. Today, that historical confusion has been compounded as many nations seek to reestablish their ancient names.

Some, like the Assiniboine and the Mandan, are straight-

99

forward and singular. For others, two names are used synonymously. Shoshone and Snake are one and the same. Sioux is a collective for the largest and best known of the plains nations, a term which holds within it the names of a welter of individual bands, many of them as well known as the catchall. The Yankton, Teton, Hunkpapa, Sans Arc and Brulé are all Sioux. It is the same for the Blackfeet, a general term for the loose confederacy of related tribes and bands which dominated the Milk River country and the Rocky Mountain front for more than two centuries. Here the confusion of names is even greater. In Canada, where the confederacy was known by the general term Blackfoot, it included the *Siksika* of the Bow River, the *Kainai* of the Oldman River Valley and the North Piegan of the Crowsnest hills. Below the border, they are the Blackfeet, often referred to as the South Piegan and by their own name, *Pikuni*. Often included (and confused) with the Blackfeet were the Atsina. Occupying the southern boundaries of the Blackfeet lands, they were a distinct nation with ancient ties to the Arapaho of the southern plains. The Atsina would become better known by the less-than-charming name of Gros Ventres, or big bellies.

The names of the nations which etched and painted the myriad renderings of animal and human figures on the soft sandstone hoodoos and cliff faces along the base of the river valley at Writing-On-Stone cannot known for certain, but consensus for their authorship seems to have settled on two probabilities. The earliest drawings are most likely Shoshone, dating from the early eighteenth century at the latest. Their renderings of sharp-shouldered figures carrying large, pre-equestrian shields turn up in some Great Basin sites known to be Shoshone. That there are no representations of either guns or horses marks them clearly as precontact.

Blackfeet oral histories tell of driving the Shoshone across the mountains by the middle of the eighteenth century (accounts confirmed by Anthony Henday when he wintered with the northern Blackfeet in 1754). It is likely the Blackfeet themselves added the equestrian images and characteristic square-shouldered figures, which also adorn their teepee covers.

Why the Shoshone and the Blackfeet left these pictures on the stone of the river valley is also open for debate. It's not surprising in these times of native cultural renewal that the brochures and guidebooks available from the park headquarters make much—I think too much—of the spiritual nature of the place. The whine of the wind through the twisted canyons and hoodoo columns might have charged this valley with a certain mystery, but it's hard to imagine these people being intimidated by any natural phenomenon. Rather, it would have served only to intensify a wonderfully nonrational joy in the place. Nevertheless, among the almost fifty sites where rock art has been identified, there is no doubt that many were created as part of some personal or collective ritual. The fantastic or mythical figures, many unidentified or too worn to read, could have come about as the result of a dream quest.

Other sites, though, are less distant and have a more immediate appeal. These places reveal a people who could express a wonderful delight in the land of which they were a part. Drawings of game and their tracks may have represented trophies, the record of an especially difficult and challenging hunt. Perhaps the ancient hunters took much the same pride in their skills as we do, practicing what amounts to visual taxidermy.

A mile east of the campground, along the Hoodoo Trail, a depiction of a battle scene is the most complex and lively example of the Blackfeet petroglyphs outside the protection of the preserve. It lies low on a sheer cliff just above the river, and were it not for the protective wooden framework built around it, most walkers on the trail would pass by without noticing. It is small—perhaps only three feet across—and the figures are lightly scratched, almost sketched, into the sandstone, but the scene swarms with a wonderful vitality.

Coming in from the right, a force of more than sixty warriors attacks a circle of teepees defended by a line of rifles. It is quick, abstract drawing, but it conveys a multitude of small details. There are horses with travois, bows and arrows, and teepee poles standing with and without their covers, one of which holds three tiny figures. In the center, along the skirmish line, a defender shoots an attacker at the precise moment he swings his hatchet.

The horses and the preponderance of guns over bows say that this is a nineteenth-century drawing. Other evidence has it to be the account of an unsuccessful attack on the Piegan by the Atsina some time after the end of their old alliance in 1860. It may even be the record of the very horse-stealing episode which broke the two nations apart. The immediacy and detail say it was probably sketched by someone who was a part of the battle, and I like to think it is the work of the rifleman who shot the hatchet bearer.

Though it is the record of a major, pitched battle, the drawing also conjures for me a gentler image of the Blackfeet. Camped along this river in a valley rich with game, chokecherry and buffaloberry, confident and relaxed in a time of plenty, a man recounts a great fight and his glorious part in it. He might be telling the story to members of other families camped nearby. Perhaps he is telling his own grandchildren. As he spins his tale, he scratches the record of his heroism into the sheltering cliff near the fire, a visual aid to his ancient oral traditions.

It's with the battle scene that I part company with those who would make every aspect of native life into some grand spiritual exercise. There is simply too much of a vigorous personality here, too much of a light touch and a lively imagination to be buried under what has become the cloying blanket of such labels as spiritual or sacred. These places are so rare that it is vital we not lose sight of, or in any way diminish, the wonderful humanity of the drawings in this valley.

How long there has been a native presence in Milk River country is not known to a certainty, but a small number of projectile points found on the north side of the river near One-four have been dated to between eight and ten thousand years ago. If the oldest estimate is correct, it probably marks the first reasonable date for human life in an area emerging from the last continental ice sheet.

Research focused on establishing exactly when humans first crossed from Asia has steadily pushed the generally accepted date back toward seventeen thousand years. There is evidence from the Yukon to support such a date, where geology and geography have joined with archeology to redraw the time line. It was axiomatic that the ancestors of the Blackfeet, the Atsina, the Navaho, the Aztec and all the rest could not have swept across this continent much before ten or twelve thousand years ago because the land was still frozen under a thousand feet or more of glacial ice. But was it? Years of detailed study into the comings and goings of the great glaciers suggest there was a way through the ice. When the glaciers poured onto the plains, they came from two directions: southwest from the high Arctic and due east out of the mountains, their leading edges blending along a line just east of the Continental Divide. As the ice began its retreat, this thin transition zone would have been the first to open, creating a narrow corridor leading from Alaska down onto the ice-free expanse of the Great Plains. Such an event could bring a native presence into the Milk River country hundreds, perhaps thousands, of years before they arrived in areas far to the north and east. Though the evidence is still slim, it does suggest a steady, seasonal native occupation along the length of the Milk River from the end of the ice until the last of the buffalo were gone.

Interpretation of the physical remnants—the few points, the stone circles and the petroglyphs—is risky, but given what we know of the historical ecology of the high plains and the pragmatism of the plains cultures, the scarcity of artifacts should not be surprising. From the time of the final emergence of what we know today as the shortgrass environment, the middle Milk River country would have been summering land, part of a regular, cyclical movement which mirrored the changing seasons and the migration of the buffalo.

Archeologists and oral traditions confirm what common sense would seem to make obvious: that any attempt to overwinter on the open plains would have been an act of supreme recklessness. Winters were for the transitional margins and the higher ground, for the foothills and sheltered valleys with their protection from the wind and snow, their firewood and their steady supply of water. In winter, the bands would separate and settle into the wooded valleys in numbers which the valleys could sustain. Demands on firewood and, after the coming of the horse, on grazing lands would be too great to support more than close family groups. The buffalo would be there, too, along with the deer and the elk, their great summer herds subdivided into the hills, hunkered down and moving only as the supplies of grass and water dictated.

As spring came, the individual families moved onto the plains again. The South Piegan came north and east from the Marias River and the Sweetgrass Hills, the Atsina up from the Bears Paws, the Plains Cree and Assiniboine down from the Cypress Hills, all following the buffalo as they drifted toward the heart of the Milk River country. Allied bands would meet and merge for the great spring hunts, replenishing everything the long winter had worn out, including themselves. If at any time life was easy on the high plains, it was April and May, a time of physical and spiritual rebirth, a time for ceremony and celebration. Late spring and early summer would have seen the nations drawn together in their greatest concentrations.

As summer deepened and the plains dried out, the bands would once again begin to disperse and retreat toward the margins. Late summer and fall were for hunting for meat and for robes, for drying and smoking and tanning, for building stores to be dragged slowly back into the sheltering valleys. This steady, predictable rhythm held for thousands of years.

While no white man had seen the Milk, the Musselshell or the Judith until Lewis and Clark named them in 1805, the impact of white culture on the tribes which inhabited the heart of the continent had been enormous. It can barely be contemplated. Before either had met the other face to face, the European presence in North America had sown the seeds for the brief flowering of the brilliant horse cultures of the plains Indian.

If there is a simple, unifying image of the Great Plains cultures, it must be the Indian mounted on a Spanish horse, brandishing an English musket. Should that seem facile, it is crucial to remember that when La Salle made his huge claim to the deepest heart of the continent in 1682, neither the horse nor the gun had reached the northern plains. Within two centuries, the life which these two things made possible had grown, flourished and all but disappeared.

Neither the horse nor the gun created what we think of as the Great Plains cultures, for the changes they wrought were quantitative, not qualitative. All the elements, all the instincts, had been present for thousands of years before the Spanish first stumbled onto the continent. What the horse and, to a lesser extent, the gun allowed was their full articulation. The horse gave to a nomadic people the thing which finally meant survival itself: mobility.

Native use of the horse spread steadily north and east from the Spanish colonies around the Gulf of Mexico and did not reach the most northern of the plains tribes—those between the Missouri and the North Saskatchewan—until after 1700. As each successive tribe obtained this priceless commodity and learned about its use, care and breeding, the whole dynamic of life on the plains changed. Those who took to the horse flourished and prospered; those who did not had already been eclipsed and were in serious decline by the time Lewis and Clark came up the Missouri.

Just as the true plains are a single, unified environment— flat, semiarid and treeless—so the first peoples to inhabit them shared several characteristics which marked them as different from those who surrounded them on three sides. The plains Indians were nomadic and mostly nonagricultural because the buffalo were nomadic and because these lands were largely ill-suited to even small-scale farming. Their weapons—the spear and the bow—were specifically adapted to the hunting of big game, and in their need to move with the great herds of buffalo, the plains nations became the only peoples south of the

Arctic to use beasts of burden (first the dog and then the horse). Unlike those nations which surrounded them, the plains Indians were people of the land, not of the water. Their rivers were largely unreliable—changing with the season from full flood to nearly bone-dry—and they flowed in the wrong direction, heading west to east at right angles to the great buffalo migrations. Wherever plains Indians needed to go, they walked, carrying or dragging all they owned.

Before the horse, life on the northern plains would have been lived along the razor's edge of survival. To stand today anywhere on the open grasslands is to see the severe limitations which the land imposed on the peoples who had chosen to live there: the transitory supplies of fresh water, the alkaline ponds and infrequent rainfall, the annual temperature extremes which are the greatest anywhere on the continent. A scarcity of shrubs and trees for firewood and shelter also meant the lack of their fruits or nuts to supplement the diet. Though game was not scarce over much of the plains, it was, with the exception of the comparatively slow and predictable buffalo, extremely wary, blindingly fast and difficult to hunt. It was the buffalo, and only the buffalo, which made life possible for the peoples of the Great Plains.

It was a hard life which bred a fierce and jealous spirit without room for the social pleasantries which the perpetual abundance of the coasts allowed. There was little opportunity to generate any surplus which might represent wealth or the basis for a complex trading network. All held the same few essential possessions, all depended on the same limited resources and peaceful coexistence was a luxury they could not afford.

The horse did not breed the ferocious tenacity of the

plains peoples, but it magnified it and gave it its fullest expression. With the horse, the tribes' mobility increased and their hunting and raiding territories expanded. The number of possessions they could afford to keep and move with them multiplied. Their wider ranges brought them into more regular and intense competition with other tribes, increasing and protracting conflicts. Raiding, once essential for simple survival, became a more intricate exercise in the assertion of territorial primacy and the acquisition of wealth, which came to be measured primarily by the horse itself. The horse redefined the tribal affiliations, lit the fuse on long-standing hatreds and provided the yardsticks against which success in all things would be measured.

The horse, too, made the individual plains cultures more complex. The keeping of horses, acquired either by breeding or theft, not only made greater mobility possible, it required it. Horses needed fresh pastures to graze and water to drink every day. They also needed saddles and pack frames, halters and constant guarding against the raids they regularly provoked. The increasingly effective acquisition of basic necessities, coupled with the more complex needs of the society, drew small bands together into larger units, and the absolute number of individuals the plains could support also increased dramatically.

Almost as soon as they acquired their horses, many of the plains tribes began the specialized breeding which their new lives required, emphasizing the particular traits essential for the war pony, buffalo runner or pack animal. The horse as a measure of wealth also brought with it a new meritocracy as those who were the best breeders, hunters or thieves achieved an easily recognizable status within each band.

The relationships among the northern plains tribes and

those from the intermountain valleys who periodically came over the divide were, to the whites who first sought to understand them, a hard-to-fathom amalgam of cooperation and mayhem. The Milk River country was one of those places where the changing nature of native life was played out to its fullest.

From where it is born at the base of the front ranges, the Milk flows through what was the very heart of Blackfeet territory. To the east, the Sweetgrass Hills clearly "belonged" to the Blackfeet and the Atsina. Still farther east and a little to the north, the Cypress Hills marked the western edge of Assiniboine and Plains Cree lands. Possession of the lands between those two poles, between the promontory points of the Sweetgrass and the Cypress Hills, was open to question if not to discussion. While the plains nations may not have had a sense of land ownership in the same way that whites did, their grasp of such supposedly European geopolitical concepts as control or spheres of influence was by any measure sophisticated.

Any band of any affiliation was welcome to hunt the buffalo, the wolf or the grizzly anywhere between the Sweetgrass and Cypress hills. No permission was needed; no common interest truces were negotiated. Anyone could hunt the Milk River country, but to do so was to accept a set of conditions so fundamental they were probably subconscious. The rules of engagement were simple and unwavering: the farther you were from your home ground and the smaller your party, the more likely you were to be raided, robbed and possibly killed.

The horse was perfectly suited to such lightning, guerrilla strikes. The European idea of laying siege to a village or of moving thousands of men and munitions supported by wagonloads of supporting players announcing their arrival with drums and flourishes would simply not work on the plains. Not only were the territories too vast and the nomadic inhabitants too thinly spread, but the concept of all-out warfare as the Europeans understood it would have struck the Blackfeet as bizarre. For them and other plains nations, the idea was not to wipe the enemy from the face of the earth and seize his territory. Rather, it was to use the enemy as a source of wealth (horses, guns or whatever), ego gratification or religious ritual.

Warfare, like every other aspect of life on the plains, was enormously pragmatic. When the numbers were nearly equal, a raid could be postponed until the odds improved. When guns or horses could be more easily obtained through trade than through hostility, trades would be made (though, if the circumstances were favorable enough, the trade goods could be raided back the next day). Lewis and Clark's hopes for an enduring peace among the northern plains nations were hopelessly naive in face of this sort of overarching practicality.

When the Corps of Discovery came up the Missouri, the impact of the horse in the intermountain West and the encroaching white settlements to the east had already upset the natural nomadic movements of the Great Plains nations. The Milk River country was especially rich in complex and shifting relationships among tribes both resident and transient.

The Shoshone, related by language and geography to the southern Comanche, Ute and Kiowa, were among the earliest of the tribes on the western edge of the plains to obtain horses in any substantial number. With them, they expanded quickly to the north and east in the late seventeenth century, hunting the buffalo herds, terrorizing the still-unmounted Blackfeet and drawing the record of their exploits onto the rocks of Writing-On-Stone. They were certainly the resident western power above the Missouri and in all likelihood hunted and raided up across the Milk as far north as the *Siksika* villages along the Bow and the South Saskatchewan.

At some time in the first few decades of the eighteenth century, the Blackfeet, with their new horses (likely captured from the Shoshone themselves) and their first guns (from the British via the Cree and Assiniboine), began to push back. In the face of the combined weight of the horse and gun, the Shoshone collapsed back across the divide, and the power of the Blackfeet nations on the northwestern plains would remain unchallenged for nearly a century.

The Assiniboine also had recently emerged as a plains power and fancied themselves middlemen in the prospering trade between the British and the western tribes of the upper Missouri. Protective of that relationship, they were in no hurry to offer much in the way of detail to assist Lewis and Clark. For their part, the captains considered the Assiniboine to be "British" and made few offers of gifts, especially not the highly prized American medals and flags.

The Assiniboine are Sioux speakers, the only representatives of that diverse language group presently living in Canada. They share with the Sioux a common ancestry of life lived not on the plains but in the woodlands close by the Great Lakes in present-day Minnesota and Wisconsin. In the early seventeenth century, the Sioux nation divided and began to move.

As the main body pushed south, the emerging Assiniboine went north. By the middle of the seventeenth century, Jesuit priests were identifying them as a separate tribe already moving west toward Lake Winnipeg. The Assiniboine were among the first of the nations west of the Great Lakes to trade with the Hudson's Bay Company (and with the French) for the guns, kettles and metal knives. Allied with the Cree on their northern flank, they divided and subdivided into groups that pushed up the South Saskatchewan as far as the mountains and to the south onto the Great Plains of the Dakotas and eastern Montana, taking most of what was west of the Mandan for their own.

Their long-standing alliance with the Cree marked the Assiniboine as a diverse nation which defined the hybrid margin between the emerging horse cultures to the south and the woodland canoeists of the north and east. Inveterate traders, they were the conduit through which such nations as the Blackfeet obtained their first guns and other manufactured items long before they were forced to deal face to face with the whites.

In the West, the Milk River country marked the shifting border between the Assiniboine and the Blackfeet Confederacy. The Cypress Hills, as much as they were anyone's, belonged to the Assiniboine; the Sweetgrass Hills did not. South and west of the Assiniboine, between the Missouri and the Milk, were the Atsina. Though closely tied to the Blackfeet (sharing their ancient Algonquian language and their general dislike of the white traders), the Atsina were not native to the northern plains. At some time in the not-so-distant past they had separated from the main body of their nation, the Arapaho of the Colorado–Nebraska country. Their movements might have been a consequence of the westward expansion of the Crows or the Cheyennes or simply the result of a widening search for better hunting territories. But the Atsina came north. When the Corps of Discovery and the early American fur traders came up the Missouri, the Atsina ranged along the Milk and the Missouri at the eastern edge of the Blackfeet lands. If any nation could be said to have owned the country below the arc of the Milk River, it would have been the Atsina.

Compared with those who surrounded them, the Atsina were a small nation. Their survival on the northern plains was due to a combination of fierce independence tempered by dexterous diplomacy. Their close alliance with the Blackfeet probably extended back to their earliest days along the Missouri and survived until well past the middle of the nineteenth century. They were the only nation which seemed consistently able to get along with the Blackfeet, and they ranged throughout Blackfeet territories as if they were their own. Though most early traders and trappers considered the Atsina to be an integral part of the Blackfeet Confederacy, they nevertheless seemed able to recognize them as a distinct group and rarely confused them with the Blackfeet proper. When the first American treaties with the northwestern plains tribes were negotiated in 1855, the Atsina and Blackfeet signed as one.

The Atsina's close relationship with the Blackfeet continued until about 1860, when a dispute over stolen horses ended it with a vengeance. The pragmatic, diplomatic Atsina quickly allied themselves with the Assiniboine, a nation with which they now share the reservation at Fort Belknap on the lower Milk River in Montana.

Though the Blackfeet, Assiniboine and Atsina dominated life along the upper Missouri, other nations were drawn to its rich hunting grounds. The Kutenai—now of the northern intermountain country of British Columbia, Idaho and Montana—hold that theirs was once a life lived fully on the plains. If so, they too, like the Shoshone, may have been driven back by the growing power of the Blackfeet. One legend even holds that in some distant past the Piegan were Kutenai. Some linguistic affinities apparently exist, but the connections are arcane and, like so much else, uncertain.

Another of the hybrid intermountain cultures to range along the Milk was the Pend d'Oreille, their presence remembered in tribal memory into the middle of the nineteenth century as they alternately camped and fought with both the Piegan and Assiniboine. Though claims for a more permanent, precontact presence are unproved, the old post office at the south end of Pakowki Lake was called Pendant d'Oreille for them, and their name survives, too, in the corruption Pondera, the northern Montana county which straddles Interstate 15 between Shelby and Great Falls.

The Nez Perce, Shoshone and Flathead came east across the divide, too, but they did so at their peril. Their hybrid life, a mix of plains and plateau culture, brought them out of their mountain valleys on annual hunting expeditions for the buffalo, but when they moved into Blackfeet country, onto the upper Milk or the Marias, they did so in force. Superior numbers would protect them from wholesale slaughter, and the few horses or lives that might be lost to sporadic, flanking raids had to be weighed against the absolute necessity of filling their larders.

All these peoples (and how many others we will probably never know) made their lives in these lands. The pictures at Writing-On-Stone, rich and varied as they may be, can only reveal the merest shadow of the complex vitality that once filled every corner of the Milk River country.

It's curious that James Doty, a careful and detailed observer of the country through which he was traveling, seemed so singularly unimpressed with this place. Even today, more than a century after he saw the petroglyphs and pictographs in their pure, unvandalized state, they still give the cliffs a strange and wonderfully evocative resonance. For Doty, though

The Writings, whatever they once were, are now nothing more than a range of Sandstone rocks thirty to sixty feet in height, parallel to the river and distant one quarter of a mile. They are worn by the action of the weather into a thousand fantastic shapes, presenting in places a smooth perpendicular surface carved with rude hieroglyphics and representations of men, horses, guns, bows, shields, etc. in the usual Indian style. No doubt this has been done by wandering war parties, who have here recounted their "coups" in feats of war, and horse stealing, in the same manner as they are often seen painted on their "Medicine Robes", and the lining of lodges.

There are other scratched drawings and paintings all over the Milk River Valley. Away from the park, they are hidden in countless coulees, perhaps discovered by a rancher out checking his cattle and known only to him or a few historians and anthropologists. Countless thousands more have no doubt already disappeared, erased by the scouring of wind against soft sandstone or lost with the crash of a bluff undercut by a flash flood. There are occasional surprises in the park, too. Despite the years of careful study and documentation, a sudden heavy rain can still wash beads or other trinkets out of the rocks, tantalizing the finder with thoughts of what might still be hidden deep in some undiscovered crevice just a few yards away.

It happens less frequently now along the Hoodoo Trail and back in the archeological preserve, but discoveries continue to be made across the river in the less-traveled coulees. I heard talk from the locals that skeletal remains had recently sluiced out onto the floor of Police Coulee in the same place a skull had come to light many years before. A few years ago, the bones would have become macabre souvenirs; today, the park staff will consult with Blood or Piegan elders about an appropriate reburial.

Written on the soft and transitory medium of eighty-million-year-old sandstones, the petroglyphs and ochre paintings can survive no longer than the forces of wind and water will allow. It might take a hundred years, or even a thousand, but eventually they will all disappear, victims of the slow, steady erosion that constantly shapes and reshapes the Milk River Valley.

Today, the campground at Writing-On-Stone probably plays host to more people in a summer month than saw the petroglyphs in the full century between Doty's visit and the creation of the park. But in the decades before the whites came to take this country as their own, this valley would have resonated with a complexity and vitality which the weekend campers can only guess at as they wonder at the meaning of what is written on these ancient stones.

Far now from all the bannered ways
Where flash the legions of the sun,
You fade—as if the last of days
Were fading, and all the wars were done.
—EDWARD ARLINGTON ROBINSON

TRACKS & TRAILS

Milk River's big grain elevators—the United Grain Growers, the P & H and the Alberta Wheat Pool— are about the only things in town west of the tracks. They are served by the Canadian Pacific Railway, which connects the border crossing at Coutts with Lethbridge, about fifty miles north. The grain elevators did not figure when this track was first laid between Lethbridge and Great Falls, Montana. In 1889, it was Canadian coal from the Oldman River Valley that built and powered the railroad.

When the Canadian Pacific bent northwest out of Medicine Hat, choosing Calgary and the Bow River to cross the divide rather than the more southerly route through the Crowsnest Pass, it left Lethbridge with plenty of coal and no ready markets outside the small, local communities. In 1889, after the narrow-gauge Turkey Track railway began to move coal to the CPR main line at Dunbow, near Medicine Hat, the successors to Alexander Galt's North-West Coal & Navigation

Company applied to build a narrow-gauge line from Leth-bridge to Fort Benton and Great Falls. The track was built to the border from both directions, and in mid-October 1890 it was ready to deliver Lethbridge coal to the booming smelter town of Great Falls.

The narrow tracks lasted until 1900 when the Montana sec-tion was bought by the Great Northern Railway and converted to standard gauge. The Canadian narrow-gauge survived until 1911 when it was acquired by Canadian Pacific. Today, the tracks serve the grain elevators, feedlots and oil fields, moving a mix of cross-border freight up to the main lines at Lethbridge. South of Coutts, the bold green and white locomotives of the Burlington Northern carry the cross-border freight south to it own east–west main lines at Shelby and Great Falls.

When those first snorting steam locomotives rolled the two hundred miles between Lethbridge and Great Falls, they ran on tracks spiked into the old Whoop-Up Trail, finishing once and for all that first rough, brief era of white settlement along the eastern slope of the Rockies. When the boundary surveyors and the Mounties first made their way onto the Canadian high plains, they came into a country dominated by the Americans from their trading center at Fort Benton. Indeed, it was precisely to counter that domination that they had been sent west.

The fur trade and the great falls of the Missouri combined to make Fort Benton the center of the earliest settlement on the northern tier. Riverboats, at first poled or man-hauled and later powered by steam, provisioned the trade in beaver pelts and buffalo robes and carried the bounty back to St. Louis. They could go no farther upstream than the confluence of the Teton and the Marias with the Missouri, and from the early

1830s almost until the end of the century, a succession of forts and trading posts flourished and faded along the alluvial flats. Fort Benton, the last and the largest of the forts, was founded in 1846. By then beaver were scarce, and the fort existed to serve the growing buffalo robe trade with the Blackfeet and Assiniboine. Through the 1850s and 1860s, shipments leaving the Benton wharves averaged twenty thousand hides a year, a number which continued to grow into the 1870s, peaking in mid-decade at a staggering seventy-two thousand. Ten years later, the buffalo were gone and the trade in robes was just a memory.

As the buffalo trade wound its bloody way toward oblivion, the prospectors and miners of the Montana gold rush pumped new life into the fort, as did the early ranchers and the first uncertain settlers. The old network of fur and robe trails which focused on Benton saw a new, heavier, one-way traffic as ten thousand miners and the goods they relied upon moved out from the Missouri on a stream of ox-drawn wagon trains.

The notorious Whoop-Up Trail was first a prospectors' trail winding northwest from Fort Benton toward the Crowsnest Pass, connecting with the Old North Trail that ran along the foothills all the way north to Fort Edmonton. Through the 1860s, a succession of Montana prospectors explored probably every mile of the front range country between the Marias and Bow rivers, but they found little to excite them. It would be whiskey, not gold, that sustained Montana's interest in the country north of the border.

Fort Whoop-Up, a few miles west of present-day Lethbridge, lived its brief, brutal life on the buffalo robe trade, exchanging the traditional sugar, tea, knives and guns for the hides of buffalo, wolf and bear. Profits had always been solid, but introducing whiskey into the equation pushed the margins to spectacular levels, and the insatiable native taste for the stuff eventually made it almost the sole item of exchange.

There were sound reasons for the whiskey trade to move north across the border in the late 1860s. The steadily increasing demand for robes certainly forced the Montana traders to widen their search. Gold prospectors, the increasing presence of American soldiers and another serious outbreak of smallpox had combined to make the resident natives nervous and unstable customers. North of the line, the Hudson's Bay Company continued largely ignoring the Blackfeet trade. Most important, the U.S. government began to enforce its old law against trading liquor on the reservations, and it had the troops in place along the Marias and Sun Rivers to back its prohibition. Indeed, it was the presence of the cavalry along the eastern slope of the Rockies which determined the route of the Whoop-Up Trail: the shortest distance to Canada without crossing Blackfeet land.

Fort Whoop-Up and the network of smaller, less-prominent posts did not last long—five, perhaps six years at best—but their presence north of the line as riotous outposts of American business was a major factor in accelerating a process of possession and control which had begun seven years earlier with Canadian Confederation.

While closing Whoop-Up was the ultimate goal of the Mounties' long march west, it did not provide the defining moment in the closing of the last frontier. That dubious distinction goes to another trading post at the end of another trail up from Fort Benton into the Cypress Hills. The story of what happened there in June 1873 has been chronicled many times, and though the finer details may differ with each telling, the consequences of that day's bloody events are in no doubt.

In mid-May, a party of Americans bedded down near the
Teton River for one final night on the plains before following
the Whoop-Up Trail the last few miles to Fort Benton. Some
have claimed they were whiskey traders returning to the fort
from a winter of collecting robes and pelts. More likely they
were wolfers, who lived by skinning out wolves and any other
fur-bearing predators which died from eating the strychnine-
laced baits they spread indiscriminately across the plains.
Whatever else they might have been, that night they were
drunk, too drunk to secure their last camp, and it cost them
eighty horses. Who stole those horses is also open to speculation. They could have been from any one of a half-dozen
tribes, but at the time the honor was given to a small band of
Plains Cree raiding well south and west of their traditional
grounds. Whoever they were, they had probably run their
prizes north across the border before the hung-over, foot-sore
wolfers could haul their cargo the ten miles or so into Benton.

One can imagine how the party would have been greeted as
it staggered into the fort, embarrassed before a population of
experienced trappers and traders who would know they had
been the agents of their own humiliation. Remounted and rein-
forced, with the hoots of the Bentonites still ringing in their
ears, John Evans and Thomas Hardwick led their men northeast toward the border and the Cypress Hills, intent on recover-
ing their property. Somewhere above the line they lost the scent
and headed straight into the hills, bound for the small trading
posts of Abel Farwell and Moses Solomon. What they found
was neither their horses nor the Cree, but a weak, sad collection
of about two hundred Assiniboine. Half-starved from a hard
winter camp in the Battle River country to the north, the band,
led by Little Soldier, had barely survived their spring migration

into the sheltering Cypress Hills. With few horses and fewer rifles, they were a gaunt shadow of what had once been a proud, fierce nation.

No one knows who drank the most bad whiskey on that night at the beginning of June or who fired the first shots the next morning along what we now call Battle Creek. The truth was lost from the start in the charges and counter-charges and self-serving politics on both sides of the border which distinguished the "firsthand accounts" in the newspapers of Fort Benton, Helena and Ottawa. What is known is that when the wolfers rode back out of the Cypress Hills, still without their lost horses, they left behind one of their own together with the mutilated remains of Little Soldier and more than thirty of his band.

When the *Ottawa Citizen* broke the story in central Canada, it was written as a case of unprovoked murder. In the *Fort Benton Record*, it became a tale of self-defense against belligerent natives, and this difference of opinion held for the two years it took to bring the wolfers to an extradition hearing in Helena. Ultimately, the effort failed. North of the border, "reasonable doubt" about the evidence eventually acquitted the three members of the party who had been arrested and charged in Canada. Nevertheless, for nearly everyone except Little Soldier and his Assiniboine, the slaughter in the Cypress Hills could not have come at a more fortuitous time.

The Cypress Hills Massacre was far from the only bloody confrontation between the old and the new ways. Just three years earlier, the U.S. 2nd Cavalry had left nearly two hundred Blackfeet dead in their winter lodges along the Marias River. In the months before they led their men into the Cypress Hills, both Evans and Hardwick had been involved in a series of deadly random skirmishes involving not just the Assiniboine, but the Crow, the Sioux and the Blackfeet as well. There must have been dozens of other minor battles which went unreported. What turned the Cypress Hills Massacre into one of history's flash points was its perfect timing, which galvanized the Canadian government into immediate action.

For nearly two centuries, the great ellipse of the Milk River country had remained a quiet eye in the swirling storm of imperial aspirations, both native and white. Change did leach into the country—the horse and the gun, the explorers, the trappers and the smallpox—but it came slowly at first, building its cumulative effect in small increments. When the attention of the wider world was finally and inevitably focused on this quiet place, its interest was drawn not to what this country was, but rather to where it was, and massive changes hit the Milk River almost literally with the speed and power of a locomotive.

Milk River's fifth flag, the ensign of the Hudson's Bay Company, had flown over this country since the border had been drawn along the 49th parallel in 1818. The resident though largely indifferent manager of these British territories, the company had retained its control even after the creation of Canada in 1867. Though Confederation itself had no measurable impact on the few souls who inhabited the Milk River country at that time, it cast the die for the transformation of the place, which began its riotous course with the beginning of the next decade.

In 1870, the Hudson's Bay Company sold its ancient rights in Rupert's Land to the new Canada, abandoning along with the Milk River its long-dormant aspirations to the Missouri River country. When, one year later, British Columbia entered Confederation, Canada finally rivaled the United States in its unbroken dominion over lands stretching between the Atlantic and the Pacific. It was British Columbia's belated joining with Canada which first drew Ottawa's attention to the broad horizons of its new western lands. The bribe to bring the Pacific into the fold had been the promise of a transcontinental railway, which would traverse the increasingly dangerous country between the Saskatchewan River and the border.

Plans to bring the southern prairies firmly under Canada's new national government had been around even before the moment the company relinquished its claim, but they had either languished under indifference or been shoved aside by the more immediate demands of a succession of railway-bred scandals. Then the vigilante wolfers came up across the border looking for their horses.

Hardwick and Evans' brutality managed to focus the attention of national governments on both sides of the border squarely on the Milk River country. For Ottawa, it was a matter of sovereignty. How long would it be before the U.S. cavalry crossed the line on some punitive mission or another? The published stories of Hardwick and his men wreaking their drunken revenge on otherwise peaceful Canadian Indians was sure evidence that the border must be secured against American interests. In Washington, too, there was support for a Canadian military presence along the line. Efforts to subdue what Americans liked to call "the hostiles" and the traders who kept them drunk and unruly could hardly be effective as long as there was easy sanctuary along their northern flank. There was simply too much country for the cavalry to cover.

Once Canada decided to take genuine possession of its southern plains, the changes came with almost unbelievable speed. In combination with the other forces already at work, the country was transformed in barely a decade. Only twelve months after the Cypress Hills Massacre, the surveyors and astronomers of the boundary commission had built their cairns along the 49th parallel all the way to the Great Divide. On the way back to their Manitoba camps in the late summer of 1874, they encountered a contingent of the newly formed Mounted Police coming west along their trail. The commissioners sold the police the surplus oats they would need to get their horses across the driest heart of the country.

By the end of that year, the Mounties would be settled at Fort Macleod, firmly planted at the head of the Whoop-Up Trail. Within another twelve months, forts were under construction at Calgary and at Fort Walsh in the Cypress Hills, and scarlet tunics were becoming a familiar sight everywhere along the north side of the border.

By the fall of 1877, Treaties 4, 6 and 7 had brought the whole of the Canadian high plains nations under the patronage of the British Crown. By then, too, the first of the cattle it would take to feed the newly dependent nations were already grazing on the foothills grasslands. Just two months after the tenth anniversary of the Cypress Hills Massacre, the tracks of the Canadian Pacific Railway had reached across the plains and into the small police fort town of Calgary.

Through it all, Fort Benton and its flexible entrepreneurs south of the border remained the commercial center of the northern tier. For more than half a century, its merchants and traders steadily took advantage of one new opportunity after another, moving easily from beaver pelts to buffalo robes, from prospectors' picks and pans to whiskey, pots and guns. When the boundary surveyors and the Mounties needed hay and oats for their horses, they came to Fort Benton. When the growing settlements north of the line needed lumber, sugar and flour, the Benton traders could supply it in tremendous volume. When the government needed cattle to feed its new wards on the great reserves, Americans I.G. Baker and the Conrad brothers would drive them north. Where Fort Benton traders' carts had once brought buffalo robes south from Forts Walsh and Macleod, they now carried loads of Oldman River coal. Until the railway gave Canada an east–west route for its cattle and wheat, the ox-drawn wagons of the Benton traders ensured that Alberta's borderlands retained their profoundly American character.

Fort Walsh lasted less than a decade. Built in 1875, abandoned and then torn down in 1883, it was here precisely as long as it took to drain the sorry, drunken spirit out of the Cypress Hills. It was here that Sitting Bull came to plead his case for peace and sanctuary. Chief Joseph, with the same thing in mind, got close enough to see the cool, dark green of its sheltering pine forests. Though a whole mounted garrison of officers and men ranged east and west through the Milk River country from the fort, it was here that the cherished Canadian image of the lone Mountie subduing the Custer-bloodied Sioux was born.

Today, out at the end of the eastern trail, Fort Walsh has been reconstructed, given a visitor center, lots of signs and summertime interpreters in period costumes. The site along Battle Creek is still a gentle break between the wooded heights of the Cypress Hills and the parched grasslands which stretch away south toward the Milk and the Missouri. Its status as a national historic site will ensure that this place and what it means will survive far longer than the original fort.

Abel Farwell's trading post has been reconstructed as well.

A small, sod-roofed jumble of isolation, it's a sharp counterpoint to the peace, order and good government written all over Fort Walsh a mile or so away up Battle Creek. Post and fort are bound to each other in this beautiful valley, a perfect expression of cause and effect. Behind palisades of newish wood, Farwell's post exudes a pleasant, almost pastoral air which makes it hard to knock the romance out of it, hard to imagine the smoky, sordid, whiskey-ridden place it was. What happened here to Little Soldier and his Assiniboine is as close as Canada came to its own Marias Massacre, to its own Wounded Knee. Remembering that is important, too.

The tracks of the Fort Benton oxcarts are probably still out here somewhere, arching north by west around the Sweetgrass toward Lethbridge or running straight across the high plains toward Fort Walsh and Abel Farwell's place. Wherever the shortgrass has not seen a plow, tracks should still be visible a century after, for better or for worse, they cut the first white lifelines into the Milk River country.

*The column came at a leisurely pace, leaving a trail of
dust that blew to the south.*

—JAMES WELCH

AN AMIABLE &
HOSPITABLE
FOLK

*T*oday, the land below the Sweetgrass Hills is a wide
and empty sweep of wheat field and pasture gridded
and measured by wide-spaced gravel roads that see little traffic and few people who do not make their lives here. It
has been this way for a century now, but from these heights I
can still sense how it must have looked before the rapid-fire
events of the 1870s closed this last wild place.

Once there were only the wandering buffalo and the transient nations which shadowed them in their circular migrations
across the infinite plains. From the summits of these hills I can
look down on each of the three places which marked the end
of their lives in this country. Perhaps forty miles away to the
southwest, the Tiber Dam and the great bend of the Marias
River mark the place where, in 1870, the Blackfeet were slaughtered into final submission. To the northeast, in the black shimmer of the Cypress Hills, Little Soldier and his small band of
Assiniboine met their end at the hands of Montana wolfers

just three years later. And before the decade was out, away on the southeastern horizon beneath the slumped silhouettes of the Bears Paw Mountains, it remained only for Chief Joseph and what was left of his Nez Perce to bring an end to the remarkable horse cultures of the plains.

When the oxcarts of the Fort Benton traders first crossed this broad expanse, they paused briefly in their overnight camps, leaving only narrow tracks in the grass on their way to somewhere else. There was enough metal in these hills to draw the prospectors and keep them for a few years but never enough to trigger the high fever of a Helena or a Butte. The cattle and the grain and the roads that followed the gold seekers came later and more quietly than they did in places where the soil was richer and the rains more plentiful. Only once was the great shroud of silence in these hills broken.

In late July 1874, the northern shoulders of the Sweetgrass Hills sheltered the greatest accumulation of scientists, teamsters, scouts, cooks and soldiers to be seen above the Missouri before the coming of the railway. On the plains below the buttes, the combined forces of the International Boundary Commission— American, Canadian and British—established an astronomical station and the last of their great base camps, preparing to draw the 49th parallel across the last one hundred miles between Manitoba's Lake-of-the-Woods and the Continental Divide. In the brief weeks between the time they came into the Milk River country below Wood Mountain, Saskatchewan, and the day in mid-August when they crossed the Hudson Bay Divide and descended into the valley of the St. Mary, the party played a singular part in the end what was left of the open West. That hot, dry summer of 1874 marked the outside world's final assault on the last frontier.

Within eighteen months of the surveyors' passage, the Mounted Police had come west on their own long march and established a string of forts and outposts along the Canadian side of the new line. Within two years, most of the U.S. 7th Cavalry which had accompanied the surveyors through two seasons in the field would lie dead in the valley of the Little Bighorn. Within a decade, the buffalo would be gone, and Texas cattle would be grazing on the abandoned grasslands with the Canadian Pacific and Great Northern railways laying track toward them at breakneck speed. Still, in that summer of 1874, it was possible to glimpse the last fragments of a life which had endured on the northern plains for perhaps 150 years.

The astronomers and surveyors of the boundary commission carefully recorded their meetings and dealings with the Blackfeet and the cavalry, with the Assiniboine, Sioux, Atsina and Metis—with all the last-act players assembled along their line of march.

The boundary commission found the Metis in their summer camp below the Cypress Hills. Observing two hundred teepees of both canvas and buffalo hide, five hundred horses and numerous Red River carts, the commissioners found these hybrid buffalo hunters "semi-civilized." They "all speak French and a priest travels with them," wrote Samuel Anderson.

Sixty Assiniboine lodges greeted them at Goose Lake. The hunters seemed pleased by the idea of a boundary line to keep out the Americans, hoping it would to be a wall rather than a thin string of widely spaced cairns. Their distaste for the Americans had peaked the year before at the Cypress Hills Massacre. The Sioux were fewer in number. Riding alone or in the company of small groups of Assiniboine, they would test the strength of the commission camps and, where the odds were in their favor, help themselves to the stored supplies.

As always, though, it was the Blackfeet who commanded the richest mix of curiosity and apprehension. From their base at the Sweetgrass Hills, the commissioners rode out to visit and photograph the mummified remains of twenty scalped and mutilated River Crow who had been caught on the open plains by the Piegan. But this evidence of Blackfeet preeminence in the upper Milk River country was old and stale. By the summer of 1874, the unchallenged authority of that great nation was already beginning to fade into memory. The winter of 1870 had all but finished the Montana Blackfeet, and the commissioners had nothing to fear.

In January of that year, with the nations of the northern tier still reeling from one of the worst outbreaks of smallpox since the turn of the century, Colonel E.M. Baker led four companies of cavalry north from Fort Shaw on the Sun River. He was under orders to hit the camp of Mountain Chief in retaliation for an earlier raid on a Montana ranch which had left one white man dead and his son seriously wounded.

Drunk as usual, Baker found the wrong camp, and just before dawn on a bitterly cold morning he turned his troops loose on the lodges of Heavy Runner, a chief who had already resigned himself to peace with the whites. When it was over, 173 South Piegan men, women and children lay dead, still wrapped in their winter sleeping robes. Three hundred more, many still ravaged by the pox, were placed under arrest. On that day, the Blackfeet ceased forever to be a serious threat to the resettlement of the northern plains.

The massacre on the great bend of the Marias River wrote the sorry conclusion to the story of America's relationship with this proudest and most intractable of the high plains nations. It is a story which had its beginning on a July morning just sixty-four years earlier and perhaps forty miles to the west. On that day, Captain Meriwether Lewis first met the Blackfeet.

Disappointed by their lack of contact with the tribes of the upper Missouri, the captains undertook to widen their sphere of exploration on the return voyage from the Pacific coast. Lewis was to explore the Marias River, hoping to find a shorter, easier route between the Columbia basin and the great falls of the Missouri. On the way, he was to establish some relationship with the elusive Blackfeet.

The idea of deliberately looking for these unchallenged masters of the northwestern plains must have filled Lewis with some trepidation. It certainly seemed like a bad idea to the five Nez Perce who were guiding him at the time, and they took the first opportunity to wish the party well and turn back for home. After crossing the divide, Lewis turned north to explore the possibility that the Marias River, the Hidatsa's *Ah-mah-tah*, might offer a more direct connection to the Columbia than the three forks of the Missouri.

The encounter was far from accidental. Lewis had been instructed by President Jefferson and his scientific advisors to make contact with all the tribes along his route. He was "to be neighborly, friendly and useful to them and confer with them on the points most convenient as mutual emporiums [trading posts]." He was to try to convince influential chiefs to visit Washington and in general to lay the groundwork for the great commercial adventure which was to come. He was to learn the names of the tribes, their languages and "occupations." He was to describe their diseases, morals, customs and populations. Jefferson's friend and chief medical advisor to the Corps, Dr. Benjamin Rush, wanted to know much more: their burial rituals and their bathing habits, whether they sacrificed animals or committed suicide. Lewis was even requested to take a sampling of their pulse rates (and three times a day, no less).

While their Mandan village winter of 1804–05 had provided Lewis and Clark with rich and varied firsthand sources for their study of the aboriginals (and they had taken good advantage of them), the same could not be said for their travels on the upper Missouri. From the time they left the villages at the beginning of April until they sighted a mounted Shoshone warrior west of the divide on August 11, they saw not a single Indian.

It is difficult to comprehend that the Corps could have traveled so far and found so little evidence that the country was anything but uninhabited. It was not uninhabited. At any given time, it was reasonable to expect that they would have encountered any of twelve significant plains tribes in any number of combinations.

Knowing that the Marias was made from two main tributaries—what we now call Two Medicine River and Cut Bank Creek—Lewis aimed for the point where he had turned back the previous summer and followed the stream northwest up the Cut Bank. With recent signs of natives all around him and able to see that the gap in the mountains through which the creek flowed would not lead much farther west, Lewis gave up and turned his party south overland toward the Two Medicine and Missouri rivers.

On July 26, 1806, all the signs and rumors became flesh and bone as Lewis found himself face to face with the Blackfeet. Exactly who Lewis met is still uncertain. Near-contemporary accounts, however (like that of David Thompson in 1807), record that the party was in fact South Piegan, forefathers of the nation whose reservation lands now encompass the Two

Medicine country. Whoever they were, their first brush with the United States of America did not end well.

Lewis had heard of the Blackfeet (likely from Assiniboine visitors to the Mandan villages), and nothing he had heard would have given him much comfort as he moved upstream in 1805. As fierce and tireless in the defense of their hunting lands as they were in raiding their neighbors', the confederacy had been dramatically transformed by the horse and the gun.

Among white and native alike, the reputation enjoyed by the Blackfeet at the close of the eighteenth century did not fit with the first reports which had come back along the Saskatchewan River some fifty years earlier. In 1754, the Hudson's Bay Company sent Anthony Henday across the prairies on what amounted to a business development trip. He was to meet with the tribes in the extreme southwestern corner of the empire in an effort to convince them to abandon their ties to the French and do their trading with the Company.

As far as its main purpose was concerned, the mission was a complete failure. Neither the Assiniboine nor the Plains Cree he encountered were willing to deal with the English. Their existing trade connections were more immediate and suited their purposes. And they were plainsmen, not canoeists, and uncomfortable with the thought of the narrow, crowded horizons of the wooded parkland and rocky shield between them and Hudson Bay. Still, Henday's was a trip full of firsts.

Alone or in the brief and changing company of the various bands he encountered, Henday moved mostly on foot in an unprecedented journey west, touching the Red Deer River as well as both the North and South Saskatchewan. Though his precise wanderings are not known, he was the first Englishman to see the Rockies (supposedly from a promontory south of the present-day city of Red Deer), the first of his nation to see Indians on horseback and the first to meet the Blackfeet.

Henday spent the winter of 1754–55 among the Blackfeet, finding them "an amiable and hospitable people," but he could not draw them into trading with the distant Company. They preferred to keep their backs to the Rockies and continue paying a premium to Assiniboine middlemen for the kettles and metal knives and especially the guns so highly prized in their ongoing brawls with the Shoshone and even the Assiniboine themselves.

Henday brought the Company no new customers, and his reports of what he had seen, especially about Indians on horses, were greeted either with skepticism or complete indifference. Along with Henday's firsts, however, was a significant last. His positive report on the character of the Blackfeet would be just about the last time that any early chronicler would refer to them as anything even approaching amiable and hospitable.

Unlike the Shoshone and the other intermountain tribes for whom white men were barely a rumor before they met the Corps of Discovery, the Blackfeet which Meriwether Lewis finally encountered were well-acquainted with the French and English of the Saskatchewan River system. They had always been willing to trade buffalo or wolf skins for possessions which had already made them by far the most powerful nation for hundreds of miles in any direction.

Lewis's story of his first encounter is a detailed account of what went wrong between the Blackfeet and the American whites. It was a series of mistakes and miscalculations which would be the cause of much bloodshed for the next seventy years.

Wanting to establish goodwill among the nations north of

the Missouri, the prerequisite for the complex trading network envisioned by Jefferson, Lewis approached the Blackfeet cautiously but determinedly. The Americans, he told them, would soon be coming west in strength, establishing trading posts all the way from St. Louis to the Pacific, offering a much better deal than the British and the Assiniboine. He gave them small gifts from his dwindling supplies and even offered ten horses to whoever would come to meet with his main party at the mouth of the Marias. To all this, he records, the Indians "made no reply."

Whatever else they may have been, the eight warriors were obviously neither intimidated nor particularly impressed by their first sight of an American. Lewis, lulled by their quiet demeanor and too used to the company of the helpful Shoshone and Nez Perce, went off to sleep with a minimum of fuss about security.

At dawn on July 27, the Blackfeet made what seemed a perfectly sensible response to the presence of a small party rich in weapons and poor in preparation: they made a grab for the guns and horses. By the time the brief skirmish was over, two of their number were dead (one from a shot fired by Lewis himself), six were headed back to their distant main camp at full gallop, and the whites, with what few horses they could catch in the melee, were racing the 120 miles to the security of the Missouri. They made the journey in twenty-four hours flat.

The Blackfeet reaction to the death of two of their number was a combination of an emotional need for blood revenge and a cold, rational response to the presence of a disruptive new factor in the complex trading networks in which they played an important part. Among the first to experience the Blackfeet hostility was David Thompson. He was turned back when he attempted the crossing in 1806, but recorded that an attempt a year later succeeded only because "the murder of two Peagan [Blackfeet] Indians by Captain Lewis of the United States, drew [them] to the Mississourie River to revenge their deaths and this gave me an opportunity to cross the Mountains."

That the Piegan did gain a direct measure of revenge may have been unknown to them when they killed trapper George Drouillard in 1810 near the three forks of the Missouri. Drouillard had been with Lewis during the first fatal encounter. But more than simple retribution, the motivation for the campaign of terror against the Americans was the need to protect their vital interests in both hunting and trading.

The plan conveyed by Lewis to the Blackfeet on the Two Medicine River was, if nothing else, an acknowledgment of how little the Corps had really learned about native life in this northwest triangle of the high plains. He spoke of a string of forts in the heart of their territory and of granting the Shoshone and the Nez Perce (even the Crows) what amounted to diplomatic immunity to trade at those forts. In return for cooperation, the Blackfeet would receive what? Things which were already theirs either for the taking (from those same Shoshone) or in trade from the English, who, though untrustworthy, did not intend to build forts on Blackfeet territory or do most of the trapping themselves. The Americans, who had introduced their plan for peace and prosperity by killing two of their would-be customers, were proposing to enter the Blackfeet sphere of influence and tilt what was a most favorable balance. The ferocity with which the Blackfeet resisted that proposition would be undiminished for decades. And it would be futile.

The Blackfeet may have rejected Lewis and Jefferson out of hand, but within a year or two of the brief skirmish in the

Medicine River country, the first American entrepreneurs were already risking life and limb for a piece of the riches the northwest triangle held. Those first small, independent groups must have spent as much time avoiding the Piegan and the Atsina as they did setting their traps, and many never lived long enough to pack their pelts out to the isolated trading posts which were beginning to string out along the Missouri and the Yellowstone toward the heart of the high plains. The Blackfeet drove the first traders back from the Three Forks in 1809 and killed the representatives of the Rocky Mountain Fur Company who tried to build a fort on their lands in 1823. In the same year, the same fate befell the traders of the Missouri Fur Company, and it seemed the upper Missouri would remain a graveyard for American aspirations on the northern plains. There was talk that the Blackfeet reign of terror was directed solely and specifically at the Americans and that the furs they claimed from the dead trappers were immediately traded to the British in return for more of the guns and powder they used to protect their southern flanks.

Still, the Americans came up the river in steadily increasing numbers. By the end of the 1820s, a large, year-round trading post—what would become Fort Union—stood at the confluence of the Missouri and the Yellowstone, serving as a base for a protracted assault on the last frontier. In 1831, Chief Trader Kenneth McKenzie, who took a Piegan wife and refused to accept defeat, finally managed to coax the Blackfeet away from their foothills stronghold and onto the plains for a meeting at the fort. He used a British trader well known among them to do it and cemented his new nonaggression pact with a pompous treaty, a raft of specially minted medals and in all probability a great deal of whiskey. Within another year, Fort

Piegan stood near the confluence of the Missouri and the Marias in the heart of Blackfeet country.

The names and locations of the forts changed—Piegan giving way to McKenzie and then to Benton—and the traders' relationships with the always volatile Blackfeet were never entirely without their dangers, but once the American presence had been planted along the northern tier, it was never extinguished. The effort to cut the British out of the trade equation and establish a fur monopoly along the upper Missouri made fabulous fortunes for the traders and their companies, but it finished the Blackfeet.

The horse, the gun, the whiskey and the smallpox—this was the deadly formula which killed the Blackfeet. The horse and the gun had first brought them to unchallenged glory across the northern plains. Mobility and firepower had brought the wide-spaced bands together, increased their ability to kill the buffalo and widened their sphere of influence. When the American whites came, the Blackfeet could travel hundreds of miles to trade their new surplus of buffalo robes for the whiskey they came to crave above all else. When the whites brought the smallpox up the river to their forts, the mounted Blackfeet spread it quickly back across those hundreds of miles. In making one great Blackfeet Confederacy, the horse and the gun ensured that no part of it was immune to the plagues which time and again swept into every remote valley and campsite in the once-isolated Milk River country.

Today, the northern border of the Blackfeet Reservation stretches east for nearly sixty miles along the 49th parallel from the summertime-only crossing at Chief Mountain near the Waterton–Glacier Park boundary. Still large by reservation standards, it is a small fragment of what it once was. There was a time when the Milk was a Blackfeet river from beginning to end. There was a time when it was theirs not only by the traditional right which their power provided but by the white man's law as well. Isaac Stevens' treaty making of 1855 confirmed that all of northern Montana belonged to the Blackfeet and the Atsina. Their first reservation stretched from the mouth of the Milk north to the Canadian border and west more than three hundred miles to the Continental Divide. Its southern boundary followed the Missouri and the Musselshell deep into the heart of Montana and back to the divide. Below their western lands was a huge preserve of common ground which the Blackfeet agreed to share with all the other nations which had traditionally hunted there.

For nearly two decades, white indifference to this high plains dryland left the Blackfeet and the rest to themselves. Then in quick succession came the end of the Civil War, the gold rush, the railroads and the settlers, and the Blackfeet lost most of what the whites had let them keep. In 1873, the lands below the Missouri were taken away. A year later and the southwest boundary along the Sun River was pushed north to the Marias. In 1888, the Blackfeet "ceded by agreement" (as Washington liked to phrase it) more than seventeen million acres—everything east of the upper Marias—to provide the corridor for Jim Hill's land-subsidized Great Northern Railway. In 1896, their ancient connection with the mountain valleys was severed to create the Glacier National Park.

Today, at the Blackfeet tribal headquarters in Browning, there is a huge wall map of what's left of the Blackfeet lands. It shows an impossibly complicated mosaic of colored blocks outlining the multitude of uses which this reservation is supporting, far from all of them under the control of the Blackfeet themselves. The reservation is a patchwork of tribal parcels, oil and gas leases, federal radar installations, Blackfeet farmers, absentee ranch holdings and at least one large Hutterite colony.

All this resulted from the Dawes Act of 1877. The act was one of those things about which the most charitable of observers can only say must have seemed a good idea at the time. Clearly the reservation system was not working, and to a large number of concerned white Americans, the problem was in the continued existence of a tribal culture so clearly anachronistic in a new American century. The Dawes Act was based on the premise that if families and individuals owned their own land they would become efficient, committed farmers and eventually be absorbed into the larger society. As landowners, too, they would become eligible for American citizenship, a further challenge to ancient tribal identities. It was called allotment, and it was the well-intentioned cause of terrible troubles across nearly every reservation in Montana. If experienced farmers from east of the 100th meridian could not make a go of 160 rain-shadowed acres, why did anyone expect the hunter-gatherer Blackfeet to succeed?

Allotment, including the right of landowners to sell their parcels to anyone they wished, was delayed for twenty-five years after passage of the Act—ostensibly to protect the natives from white speculators—but when it did take effect so much was lost for so little gain. On some reservations, like the forest-rich Flathead, the lands remaining after allotment were opened to white settlement. On others, like the drygrass Fort Belknap, surplus lands were given to the tribes. On the Blackfeet reservation, large tracts of the allotted land were sold off to white farmers and ranchers.

It was the same everywhere on the northern plains. To the

south, the Crow ceded much of their land to railway development and miners' dreams, and yet they were forced east, away
from other places where the whites found value. Assiniboine
and Atsina were gathered at Fort Belknap, a rectangular reservation bordering the lower Milk between Havre and Malta, land
that had once been reserved for the Blackfeet. So it was, too, for
the rest of the Assiniboine and the Montana Sioux, who were
settled at Fort Peck along the north bank of the Missouri
below the place where the Milk joins it.

The great Montana reservations—the Blackfeet, Forts
Belknap and Peck and the smaller Rocky Boys of the Bears Paw
Mountains—define the outer limits of the Milk River country,
but the native soul of the place is gone. North of the border,
too, the country has lost its aboriginal heart as surely as it has
lost its buffalo. Bands which once ranged freely between the
Milk River Ridge and the Cypress Hills and south to the Missouri are settled into the foothills country, pinned down on
what were their wintering grounds, cut off from the broad
plains and the majestic Sweetgrass that once were their summer
homes. Slowly but certainly, the wind and the water, the plow
and the fence wire are working to erase every sign that this land
was ever anything but what is today.

In Havre the wind is constant, but two thousand years are
as close as yesterday, and we fail to look back at our peril.
—MARY CLEARMAN BLEW

HAVRE &
THE HI-LINE

Alberta 880 ends in a cul-de-sac at the cluster of customs houses just below Aden. Named for another distant outpost of the British Empire and its Middle
Eastern gulf, Aden once may have been a more substantial
place, but today it is only a postal code—TOK OAO—and there
is no sign of a general store, an elevator or anything else which
might have been a focus for the widely scattered compounds
dotting the wheat fields and pastures. Of all the fifteen ports of
entry along the border between Montana and three Canadian
provinces, this must surely be the most remote.

On a fall day, a handwritten note on the Canadian side of
the compound directs me to the American house, perhaps fifty
yards away, and a U.S. border guard appears promptly at the
sound of the engine. He is relaxed and pleasant enough, but
keeps his professional distance, and my general questions about
the place elicit polite but terse replies. That's not surprising given
that nearly all the dozen or so vehicles he sees in a day are driven

by neighbors. Not surprising either since this place is steeped in a history of whiskey traders, bootleggers and prohibition smugglers, venerable professions recently given new life by the huge cross-border difference in the price of cigarettes and liquor.

The line which runs between the two customs houses has been here, by treaty at least, since 1818. In drawing the line west from Lake-of-the-Woods, Britain and the United States traded the sensible but tangled logic of river basin boundaries for the arbitrary practicality of the pen and ruler. By then, enough was known about the high plains and their future prospects to allow for such a dispassionate act. The real fight was to come west of the divide in the battle for the course of the Columbia and the beaver-rich lands of the Oregon territory.

The 49th parallel should have pleased the Americans. While giving up their claim to the northernmost extremes of the Missouri watershed—to the apex of the Milk, the source of the Frenchman, the Poplar and not much else—they secured clear and unquestioned title to the birthplace of the Mississippi and to the full course of the Missouri proper. In a warm-up to later boundary treaties, Britain gave up much more than it gained, losing perhaps 250 miles of the Red together with the great southern loop of the Souris and the sources of the St. Mary, the Belly and the Waterton rivers in what is now Montana's Glacier National Park. With the fur-bearing riches of the Red and the Souris already tapped out, the Hudson's Bay Company, in control of the region at the time, probably didn't raise much of a fuss. Besides, its agents continued to trade as far south as Wyoming's Green River country until well into the 1830s. The northern tier of the high plains was not something that anyone would find much reason to care about for another half-century.

The Sweetgrass Hills, *Katoysis* to the Blackfeet, are the stunning centerpiece of the upper Milk River, and I can feel their
pull on every trip into this remote country. Their dark, rounded silhouettes, are visible from miles in every direction, even to
the farthest boundaries of the great ellipse of the Milk River.
Though often mistaken for the leading edge of the Rocky
Mountains, they are newer things and made of different stuff.
The Sweetgrass Hills, like the Bears Paws, are volcanic at their
heart. They are what geologists call stocks. Perhaps fifty million
years ago, long after the Rockies had come up, great blobs of
molten igneous rock pushed up from the earth's core through
the ancient sediments. What triggered these convulsions across
the northern plains is not clear, but it lacked the power to drive
the pools of magma up through the surface, and they cooled
and hardened deep beneath the ground.

Thrusting four thousand feet clear of the rolling plains,
the summits of the Sweetgrass Hills show something of where
the surface of this land once was. Harder by far than the surrounding sediments, the core of the hills resisted the millions
of years of erosion which washed the plains away, and like the
Cypress Hills, their peaks would have stood well clear of the
ice sheets that flowed south around them, *nunataks* of bare stone
floating in a sea of ice. Like the Cypress and the Porcupine
hills, too, the peaks of the Sweetgrass hold island forests of
Douglas fir and lodgepole pine, which cling to the steep sides.
These few remains of the great evergreen forests which covered
the full breadth of the high plains more than once define the
upper limits of the narrow, precise formula which made the
grasslands.

The summits are cooler and wetter than their surrounding
flats and retain conditions which would have prevailed across

the whole of the plains as each of the continental glaciers died. In the vast wetlands created along the line of the decaying ice, the trees would have been the first to recolonize the bare gravels and rolling moraines, holding out only until the land warmed and the rain shadow of the Rockies reasserted itself. Evergreens would have flourished much as they do today along the line of the great shield and along the flanks of the Rocky Mountains. The successions from ice to forest and back to grass would have been rapid, requiring only barely perceptible changes in temperature and rainfall.

Once these hills wintered elk and bighorn sheep, wolf and plains grizzly, sheltering with them the Blackfeet and the Atsina and those who came before them. Once one could look down from their summits on breaking waves of buffalo in their hundreds of thousands or watch for the approach of marauding Assiniboine or River Crow. For generations the Sweetgrass belonged to the Blackfeet, but by 1888 the more pressing needs of the gold prospectors, the railway builders and the cattlemen had pushed them west toward the Marias River and onto a remnant reservation from which they can still see the dark hills floating just out of reach on the eastern horizon.

Beyond the border crossing at Aden, the gravel of Montana 409 stretches away as straight as a die until it disappears over the saddleback between the buttes of the Sweetgrass Hills. The village of Whitlash sits about six miles below the border, cradled in the high country between the East and the Gold buttes. Once there were other "populated places" (the smallest assemblage of humanity acknowledged by the topographic maps) in and around the hills—McDermott, Kippen, Hill and Gold Butte—but they are all gone now as far as the official Montana highway map is concerned. Whitlash holds a few houses, a community center, a substantial Presbyterian church and a pressurizing station for the pipeline carrying Milk River natural gas south toward Great Falls and Billings. Only one in ten of the small pump jacks which dot the northern shoulder of the East Butte is pumping, the sign of another of northern Montana's declining oil fields.

Perhaps it is the absence of a string of proper Montana bars that is the surest sign this village, too, is slowly going the way of all the small places along the northern tier. There used to be more traffic from Canada. When transportation and the roads were less reliable and the border crossing was open twenty-four hours a day, the Albertans came to Whitlash for their holiday dances and church suppers. Today, they drive north toward Milk River and Foremost. Today, good, all-weather gravel roads connect these hills with the Hi-Line town of Chester some forty miles to the south and with Sunburst over on Interstate 15. The roads might bring a few more visitors to this lonely place, but they also give the local ranchers and farmers easy access to better shopping somewhere else.

From the crest of the saddleback, the sides of the East and Gold buttes sweep sharply toward the sky, and the smooth band of bare rock between the ragged edge of the grass and the crown of evergreens makes it seem that the buttes might have burst out of the ground only yesterday. A narrow trail switchbacks up the side of the East Butte, and through binoculars I can just make out a couple of blockhouses and a nest of low antennae ranged along the edge of the summit ridge. Whatever other purposes they may serve, it's certain that some of the antennae connect the tiny U.S. customs house at Aden with the sophisticated network of sensors and computers which now constantly monitors this longest of undefended borders. The record of the few vehicles that make the crossing at Aden on an average day is automatically added to the massive information banks, including, it occurs to me only later, my own license plate number and who knows what else.

South from the saddleback, the land falls away onto the broad, rolling plains of northern Montana. Between the crest of the ridge and the infinite horizon, only the islands of the faraway Bears Paw and Highwood mountains and the wall of the Rockies break the smooth, flat shimmer. Far below, Montana 409 winds down between the smaller, isolated intrusions of the Haystack and Grassy buttes. Their broad, surrounding pastures of dry shortgrass give way steadily to the rigid geometry of wheat fields stretching away without relief far beyond the Hi-Line, across the Marias River and all the way to the Missouri.

It has been said that if the Sweetgrass Hills were in Canada, they would be a national park, and there is more than a measure of truth in the observation. North of the line, the Sweetgrass's only ecological equivalent—the Cypress Hills—is jointly preserved as a provincial park by the governments of Alberta and Saskatchewan. Here in the Sweetgrass there is no such protection, nothing for the tourist except one small, private campground tucked into a narrow coulee high on the saddleback near Whitlash. It's a quiet spot, shady with willow shrubs and sheltered from the perpetual wind. The faded sign says it belongs to the Liberty County 4-H Club but there are few indications that it is used much any more.

The Sweetgrass Hills have been in private hands since the Hi-Line was opened to ranchers and homesteaders, and today public access to their cool, green heights is severely restricted. Ranch families share memories of summer days spent on climbs to the top of the West or Gold buttes and of autumn hunts for the deer and elk which still flourish here. Historians and archeologists are drawn here, too, scouring the caves and eroded gullies for the scattered evidence left by centuries of earlier hunters.

Prospectors and miners brought their gold fever into these hills in the few short years of near anarchy which marked the line between the end of the Blackfeet and the coming of the cattle, but their presence was brief and finally inconsequential. The village of Gold Butte once boasted a well-stocked general store, a hotel and a few saloons. It survived until the end of the second gold rush and then managed to hang on into the early 1940s when the store finally closed. Today, the prospectors are remembered only by the marks they left on the maps: Miners Coulee, Gold Butte and its long-abandoned boomtown name-sake.

Homesteaders swept into these hills, too, staking their hopes on any half or quarter section which looked like it might produce wheat. Those pitifully small parcels are gone now, as they are everywhere across the Hi-Line, consolidated into the massive, mechanized operations which are today's response to farming on these dry lands. The hills have kept their caps of evergreen, though, but it may be only logistical problems which have protected them from the loggers. Still, West Butte shows a small, rectangular tonsure cut high into its eastern crest, which may be a sign of things to come.

More than anything else, this is an enormously lonely place. The 1890 U.S. Census declared any county with a population of fewer than two people per square mile to be "unsettled." Today, more than a century later, four of the seven Milk River counties still meet that criterion. Though all around there are fences and cattle and wheat fields, hours can pass without any sign of a living human presence, without even the dust of a distant truck. On my slow, relaxed, autumn drive over the hills from the border to the Hi-Line, I met only three other vehicles. A pickup from the Firestone dealer in Chester, its bed filled with two or three huge tractor tires, came flying blind over a hill on my side of the road. I rated a grin and quick wave from a driver as surprised to see me as I was him. A dark brown delivery van from the United Parcel Service, moving away at right angles up a narrow road which seemed to lead nowhere, gave truth-in-advertising credence to the company's claim that it will go to the ends of the earth to deliver a parcel. Wherever the driver was headed, he was pushing the limits of such a promise. Another driver, at the wheel of the big Liberty County grader, slowly leveled the gravel toward the shallow shoulders and reckoned he made about five miles a day in each direction. He was a man clearly comfortable with nothing for company save his own thoughts.

The towns, or what used to be towns, along the Hi-Line string out every six or ten miles, the classic pattern of western development dictated by the team-haul principle and the need to feed and water both horse and locomotive. Some, like Glasgow and Malta, have survived and in their own way flourished. Others—the Tampicos, Vandalias and Zurichs—are down to what Dayton Duncan calls their "irreducible minimum": a post office, a general store and a few houses clustered near an elevator or a feed lot. More than these the thin population cannot support; fewer than these and the towns disappear entirely. Some used to be more; most never had the chance. All had wild hopes and impossible dreams fueled by Jim Hill and his Great Northern Railroad.

As it was north of the line in Alberta and Saskatchewan, the Milk River country of Montana was the last place to see the homesteaders' survey stakes hammered into the shortgrass. And as it was in Canada, it was the first place to see them blown away. The homesteaders ("Honyockers" as they were disdainfully called) had poured into Montana at the turn of the century, riding the Northern Pacific up the Yellowstone into the fertile Paradise Valley, the Judith basin and everywhere else there might have been a rich future on offer. The chopping up of the grassland valleys into parcels of 160 or 320 acres was frenetic, a last chance at free land. In 1909, one million acres were taken up; in 1910, four and three-quarter million. By 1913, the only potential paradise left was along the Great Northern's main line through the Milk River country.

In March of that year, the land office at Havre recorded two hundred and fifty homesteads on the first day it was open and sixteen hundred in total. It did not matter that most of the fertile bottomlands had already been taken up years before by the cattlemen or that even the three hundred and twenty acres permitted by the 1909 Enlarged Homestead Act would not keep a family alive without irrigation. Through it all, the publicity department of the Great Northern kept up its relentless campaign of blue-sky fantasy and outright falsehood.

At the outset, it appeared the Great Northern's promises might hold true. The years between 1910 and 1918 were good for most of the state. There was sufficient rain and most important a war in Europe to drive the price of wheat sky-high. In response to the years of plenty, encouraged by their bankers and implement dealers, the settlers bought up as much land as they could and borrowed to finance the purchase of combines and tractors. They used their future crops and the higher mortgage value of their land as their collateral. Then World War I ended, the rain stopped and the bubble burst.

Even had prices stood up, there would have been little wheat to sell. June 1919 was the driest month ever recorded in the state of Montana. Between 1900 and 1916, the state average for wheat production had been twenty-five bushels to the acre. In 1919, it was less than three.

The collapse that began in 1919 accelerated without relief until 1925 when things slowly began to turn around. By then, though, the damage was beyond repair. It is tempting to reel off the horrible statistics, the cold historical calculations which tell how bad it was. The whole mess is best summed up, though, in the following: Between 1920 and 1925, there were one hundred and twenty foreclosures for every one hundred farms in Hill County—more than one per farm—and, when the business was finally done by the midthirties, ninety percent of all the farm mortgages in the county had been foreclosed. The banks which held those mortgages went down as well. Nearly two hundred were buried under reams of worthless paper.

Today, there is little evidence of the tens of thousands of dryland homesteaders who flooded into the country in the second decade of the century only to be blown away by the end of the third. A few of their small shacks and outbuildings still stand along the highway and up the gravel side roads, but most were cleared away long ago, their yards and shelterbelts plowed under by the huge machines of the big wheat producers, who consolidated the inadequate homesteads into fields of a thousand acres.

The tracks the Great Northern Railway are still here more than one hundred years after they were spiked across the Hi-Line in the summer of 1887 at the record-breaking pace of

more than three miles a day. Today, the trains carry the green
and white colors of the Burlington Northern, the transportation giant created in 1969 by the merger of the Great Northern,
Northern Pacific, and Chicago, Burlington & Quincy, but in a
way it's still Jim Hill's railroad. Before his death in 1916, he held
the controlling interest in all three. The main line trains move
the wheat and cattle of the northern tier to Chicago and Seattle and return with two-story racks of Toyotas and flatcars
stacked high with Boise–Cascade plywood.

There are no more passenger trains on the Burlington
Northern, but Amtrak still runs the Empire Builder and it still
stops at Havre. Its double-deckers and observation cars may
perpetuate the name of the Great Northern's flagship stream-
liner, tracing its same route across the plains and through the
Rockies, but the shiny, antiseptic steel skin recalls nothing of
its predecessor's stunning evergreen and golden-orange paint
scheme.

Sitting midway across the state, forty miles south of Canada, Havre is the center of Montana's Milk River country.
Named for some bizarre reason after the French port city of
Le Havre (but pronounced HAV-er), its 10,200 residents make
it the biggest city on the Hi-Line by a factor of three. Created
by the Great Northern as the hub of its Montana operations,
the town has waxed and waned in rhythm with the boom-and-
bust cycles of ranching, farming, and oil and gas. Havre's last
prosperity was in the 1970s, when the futures of all those things
were coincidentally bright.

The seventies brought the free-spending fever of oil and
gas exploration, steady rains and wheat at five dollars a bushel
or better. It also brought the Holiday Village mall at the west
end of town and some new motels along Highway 2, where it

doubles as Havre's main street. As in so many western towns, oil and gas were not what we like to call sustainable development, and their effects upon Havre have now mostly evaporated. The Holiday Village mall stands a bit shabby with its back against the Milk River escarpment. The parking lot, stretching out to the highway, always looks mostly deserted, so optimistically huge that it would dwarf even a busy day's traffic. Already it is in danger of becoming an artifact every bit as representative of Havre's history as the homesteader's cabin at the Clack Museum or the Sputnik-inspired entrance to the Hill County fairgrounds.

The only hope for a growth industry in Havre these days, as it seems to be everywhere on the continent, is gambling. The only new neon signs are big and garish and stuck out in front of the only the new buildings in town: the casinos. Sadly, they may mean the permanent end to the state's most enduring and endearing part of life: the Montana bar.

The Hi-Line is not the best place to look for the great bars of Montana. They are more likely to survive on the cattleman's open range or the old mining towns along the divide. The Milk River country was homesteaded, and the hardscrabble farmer was less disposed than the cowboy or the miner to drink hard liquor, even if he had the money. The small towns along the railway were more likely to be models of practicality—churches and general stores rather than saloons and brothels—serving the day-in-town needs of the farm families, not the week-long benders of the horsemen. The timing, too, worked against the Hi-Line bar. Much of the country had barely been settled when prohibition arrived in 1918. By 1933, when Montana and the rest of America gave it up as a bad idea, the homestead wave was already a memory.

Still, there are a few good bars in Havre, bars which served as bank and hiring hall, bath house and diner, bars that were the closest thing most towns got to a community center. The good Montana bar (indeed most good bars, period) is run by one person, often the owner, except at the busiest times. Open seven days a week from 9:00 or 10:00 A.M. until the wee hours, it has a faded but still glorious back bar (the shelves, counter and such behind the bartender) imported from one of the coasts around the turn of the century. Mahogany and twelve feet high, covered with columns and carvings, its mirror has been too long in need of resilvering. The bar itself (or the plank, as it is properly called) is the perfect height for leaning elbows and deep enough to leave plenty of room for the next drink, change and cigarettes. Footrails and even built-in spittoons are not uncommon. Most bars have a selection of dusty, long-dead animals—typically elk, deer or buffalo—staring down over your shoulder. Some have become virtual museums of taxidermy, favoring along with the usual sporting game such genetic freaks as albino fawns, two-headed calves, or deer with wildly contorted racks. There's usually a place toward the back for a pool table or a Saturday night dance. Poker games were a regular staple, along with live keno, a strange variation of bingo but offering even longer odds.

Today, the plank is no longer the heart of the Montana bar—it's the video game. Walk into any of the half-dozen or more bars which line the main street of Havre and the machines are there, and sitting in front of them are rows of hunched backs, young and old. The only detectable movement is a ritualized series of small gestures as money is fed in and buttons are tapped; the only human sound is a sharply drawn-in breath followed by a quiet, mild curse. Once in a while, players will rise and cross the floor, staying only long enough to make change or pick up a fresh drink. Occasionally, they come to cash in a small win, returning immediately to their stools to begin pushing it back into the machine.

The sounds of the Montana bar are no longer laughter and the clink of glass and coin on the plank. Now, they are the incessant monotony of *beeps* and *boops* from the poker and keno machines, punctuated by congratulatory strains like those heard from a baseball park organ.

It's getting hard to find a real poker game or keno numbers being called by a human being. Even the word *casino* is deceptive. In Havre, it's just a place where there are more video terminals offering a wider variety of games, a place where the bar has shrunk to two or three stools and the bartender reduced to the status of cashier. Conversation, when there is any, is about the games, and everyone seems to have a story about someone in town who recently won big. Every small payout is celebrated as if it represented genuine profit, but by the end of the evening, most of the win, minus the cost of a couple of drinks, will be back in the belly of the machine.

The video terminals are popular and profitable, and these are tough times. Bartenders along the Hi-Line say it would be impossible to stay in business without them, though none of the older ones will acknowledge anything but disdain for their noises and flashing lights. It may be that the machines will earn enough for the owners to keep the bars open, but at what cost? It's odd and sad to think that so complex a social institution as the Montana bar might owe its life to such a profoundly anti-social device.

The Hi-Line bar is in danger of sinking into history, and history is something the Hi-Line doesn't seen to care about.

There is nothing like a serious museum or interpretive center across the entire breadth of Montana's Milk River country. Even in Havre, with its more than ten thousand people, preserving the record of what this place has been is a hit-and-miss affair driven solely by the passion of a few dedicated souls.

Without the Clack family and the devoted amateurs of the local archeological society, the *Wahkpa Chu'gn* buffalo jump would never have been saved. They built the protective shacks and sheds themselves with money taken mostly out of their own pockets. What should be a major attraction is visible only through the chain link fence behind the Holiday Village shopping mall or on one of the infrequent guided tours. North of the border, at another buffalo jump, tens of millions of Alberta oil dollars have built and promoted Head-Smashed-In as a huge tourist draw and a designated World Heritage Site.

Just south of Havre, the grand, red brick barracks and outbuildings of Fort Assiniboine are briefly visible alongside Highway 87. It has been a sprawling presence here in the shadow of the Bears Paws since 1879, the military's overkill response to the nonexistent threat of Indian trouble in the wake of the Little Bighorn and Chief Joseph's last stand along Snake Creek, just twenty miles to the east. Once the largest military reservation in America, holding the whole of the Bears Paw Mountains, this place was briefly home to a young Black Jack Pershing; to the Buffalo Soldiers, the legendary black cavalry regiment; and as one of the few historical markers takes some pains to point out, the birthplace of one John A. Burns, of all things, the Father of Hawaiian Statehood.

Though many of the outbuildings stand abandoned, windows broken and doors swinging on their hinges, the parade squares, command post and barracks with their crenellated towers are beautifully maintained, occupied for years by the Northern Agricultural Research Center of Montana State University. It is a place where serious science is being done, and there is little to indicate that visitors inquisitive about the history of the place are welcome.

It's the same story everywhere along the Hi-Line: small towns with their tiny museums, all needing the local passion of a Clack family to keep them alive. While most of the West's declining agricultural centers loudly trumpet their future in tourism, the Milk River country retains a profound disinterest in the wider world, apparently content to let the RVs sail their way west toward the mountains along Interstate 90 and 94, not deigning to make much of an effort to lure them north onto Highway 2. In some ways, it's almost refreshing to see such apathy, to see a place which has not been tainted by the rampant hucksterism of South Dakota's Black Hills or, like Big Fork and Big Timber down along the Yellowstone, pseudo-gentrified to draw in the California retirement money and the show-business ranchers.

Perhaps the people of a country who have suffered so often at the hands of the boosters are reluctant now to assume the role themselves. In these things at least, the Hi-Line retains a certain authenticity, a clearer sense of what it is than is found in other, more traveled parts of the state. But with that distaste for showing itself to the outside world, it has also become a place without a sense of its own past, without a grasp of the particulars which made it what it is.

This is a land to mark the sparrow's fall.
—WALLACE STEGNER

BREAKING
THE
PLANE

*T*he Alberta provincial park at Writing-On-Stone, created in 1957 and steadily expanded to its present forty-four hundred acres, has captured not only the wealth of more than fifty native rock-art sites along the Milk River's canyon walls but also fragments of what combined to forge the unique environment of the shortgrass prairie.

The highways leading to the park are newly paved with Heritage Fund dollars, reflecting the good-times commitment of a government both to the preservation of a unique place and to the tourist dollars which tend to avoid gravel roads. South from Highway 501, irrigated fields of alfalfa and canola and pastures of crossbred Herefords and Charolais give way at the park boundary to a wide expanse of native shortgrass.

Where the formal stone wall announces the entrance to the developed parts of the park, the road falls steeply out of sight into the valley. In the view from the crest above the hoodoos, the change from dry, windblown grass to barren, sandstone cliffs and to the dark richness of the river is concentrated into perhaps a hundred yards.

The public campground, tucked into a broad elbow along the north bank of the river at the eastern end of the park, is modern and fully serviced with a man-made sand beach, toilets and showers, a kids playground and neatly clipped grass. But in the quiet of early morning or late evening, when the mule deer come down to the river to drink, it is still possible for me to sit with my back to the campground and see across the empty valley the undulating hills of grass and sage, the cutbanks and twisting coulees which look much as they did when Lewis and Clark named the Milk River almost two hundred years ago.

On the late June weekend of my visit, perhaps a third of the seventy-five campsites are occupied with an even blend of tents, pickup campers and recreational vehicles. It has been a wet spring and the park is rich and green, alive with the birds and animals which mark this as shortgrass country. The birds of Writing-On-Stone, in their complex variety, offer any careful observer the easiest lesson in the specialized, coexistent diversity which is the essence of the plains environment. More than 160 different species have been recorded at one time or another, but fewer than half that nest in the park, the rest passing through only on their migrations or dropped here by some once-in-a-lifetime accident.

The thickets of skunkbush, wild rose and thorny buffaloberry separating the individual campsites shelter the standard southern Alberta amalgam of yellow warblers, American goldfinches and common yellowthroats, but here, in the upper reaches of the Missouri watershed, the mix is enriched by birds which are pushing the northern limits of their range.

Nesting pairs of brown thrashers stalk the lawns of the

quieter campsites along the riverbank, competing for beetles and grasshoppers with the veerys and robins. Their cocksure stride belies the nervous disposition which sends them disappearing quickly into the hedgerows if someone passes nearby. The rufous-sided towhee is common here, too, and the sweet mewling of the gray catbird pours out of the willow bushes close to the water. The yellow-breasted chat nests here as it slowly expands its range north into a province where it was first recorded only in the early 1940s. Flashing its bold chrome yellow front from the shadows of the deep thickets, this largest of all the warblers adds its loud medley of random squeaks and chuckles to the general cacophony of the early morning. Adding its name to my life-list gives me almost as much pleasure as the sight and sound of the bird itself.

Away from the comfortable artificiality of the campground and away from the river's edge, the transformation is sharp and short. In the hoodoos and shortgrass hillsides which form the valley walls, the birds and their songs change as dramatically as the land. Away from the shelter of the trees and shrub thickets, the birds take on the protective colors of the grass and the rock, their behavior adapted to a life of exposure.

Up on the plains, there is nothing like the concentrated sunrise din heard on the riverbank. Life on the uplands is lived close to the ground in the three or four feet between the earth and the tops of the sagebrush or the endless lines of fence posts. Nests are cups of fine grasses built directly on the ground, hidden at the leaf-littered base of a sage or in the thin, dense rough between the swather's blade and the fence line.

The drygrass sparrows—the savannah, the vesper and the Brewer's—are all variations on a theme of grays and pale browns, their songs a dry, insectlike buzz or a few sweet, simple notes. The longspurs—McCown's and chestnut-collared—make their summer home here on the northern edge of the plains, avoiding areas of heavy cultivation, seeking out places where the true shortgrass still survives. The scope of their range and their overall numbers may have declined, but their bold-patterned heads and flashing white tails are still a common sight where conditions suit them. As I drive south into the country, the striking white on black of the male lark bunting along the fence wire signals the transition to the drylands, its glossy color the exception to the rule of the grasslands' muted palette.

The birds of the grasslands come and go quietly, breaking from their mixed spring flocks in late April or early May to disperse across the pastures, then starting to gather again by the end of August for their migration back to the southern plains of Texas and Mexico. First to arrive—and usually last to leave—are the horned larks. Depending on the tenacity of winter, they may be here as early as the middle of February, searching for seeds along the shoulders of the gravel roads and then swirling away at the last split second to avoid a fast-moving vehicle. If the robin is the traditional harbinger in city backyards and parks, the western meadowlark announces the arrival of spring on the grasslands. Originally limited to perching on a bush or an outcropping of rock, the males now call from the tops of the fence posts and telephone poles, and their rich, short bursts of song can carry across a half mile or more.

Grasslands birds exhibit the territoriality common to most nesting passerines, but that, too, has been adapted to the limitations of the open country. In a land where trees are nonexistent, with no high point from which to announce their presence and warn away their competitors, males have taken to singing on the wing. The longspurs do it, as does the lark bunting, and John James Audubon was so taken with the dowdy little Sprague's pipit that he dubbed it the Missouri Skylark, reminded by its spiraling flight and thin, metallic trill of the little European songbird immortalized by Keats.

Between the bright colors of the bottomland warblers and the mixed browns of the grassland sparrows, the barren sandstone rocks and hoodoos of the valley walls hold their own specially adapted residents. The rock wren is here, at the northern edge of its dryland range, building its nest of grass, twigs and hair in a sheltered crevice under the rocks. In the side-by-side extremes of the coulee country, it keeps to its chosen, sun-baked place, avoiding the lush thickets and protecting trees which may be growing only a few feet away. Cinnamon and cream, like the color of the sandstones which shelter it, the rock wren moves quickly and warily after the insects on which it feeds, but its long, beautiful, burbling song gives it away at every turn.

Within the confines of the narrow valley, each species has found its niche. Sometimes different species compete over matters of common interest—defense of a territory, the best nesting sites or singing perches—but otherwise they coexist, almost oblivious to one another. So it is with the park's resident flycatchers. The rowdy, nervous eastern kingbirds nest high in the cottonwoods, bold and flashy in their sorties after the insects which drift above the river. Below them, in the willow thickets, the western wood pewee makes shorter, more furtive forays out over the same water, returning to its perch without the loud flourishes of the kingbird. On the far bank, in the dry rocks, Say's phoebe blends in with the sandstone's muted grays and browns. Patient and quiet, it flickers out over the river, unerring in its pursuit of what seems to be the one perfect insect.

In the birds of the park, one can also read in microcosm the results of modern man's presence on the high plains. Like the plants and the other animals, the birds of the Milk River Valley have both flourished and declined in response to less than a century of changing circumstance.

The longspurs stayed within their traditional ranges and as those ranges went under the plow, their numbers declined. So it has been with the long-billed curlew and the sage grouse. The greater prairie chicken is probably gone altogether, extirpated in the 1930s, though occasional, hopeful sightings are still reported.

Barns and houses and the trees to shelter them have provided new opportunities for species which would not ordinarily have strayed from the narrow river valleys. Kingbirds, both western and eastern, robins and the ubiquitous magpies and pigeons are all more numerous now than they were at the turn of the century. The wood warblers and vireos, too, might have prospered in these new niches had the destruction of their central American wintering grounds not taken away more than the "improved" plains could offer for their breeding season.

Loud and bold where there is cover close to hand, quiet and nervous in the spare shelter of the low grass, every small creature has its own place here, dividing the land with other species with invisible boundaries, staying close to ground level or, better still, well below it in the cool shadows along the coulee bottoms.

To call the shortgrass plains a single, definable environment does not deny the subtle yet enormous variations within that unified field. At the edges, in the ecotones where the plains evolve into mountain or parkland, sage and greasewood mingle with and then give way to lodgepole pine and trembling aspen. In the heart of the plains, small variations in elevation or the presence of permanent water create microenvironments as large as a fifty-mile coulee or as small as the few square yards around a natural spring.

With two glorious exceptions, life has been closely organized around small havens from sun and wind, around water and sheltering thickets. The buffalo, following the changing seasons in their great, circular migrations, once joined the endless horizons. The buffalo are gone from the open range now, gone with the oceans of grass that linked the coulees and creek beds. Today, only the great hawks survive as the last creature to connect all the small places into one as surely as their gravity-defeating flight has always been the only thing to connect the land to the sky.

Later in the same summer, another birding trip takes me north of Del Bonita, where Highway 62 dips to cross the North Milk before climbing to the crest of the ridge. My trip comes to a sliding stop on the narrow shoulder. It's an early morning full of pale sunlight, and what stops my drive are five distinct silhouettes standing quietly in a stubble field just off the road. They do not seem bothered by the benign, boxy shape of my truck, but the recognition of a human figure emerging from it sends the closest of the birds coasting back toward its companions on two or three calm, strong wingbeats. That these are buteos is obvious (too small for eagles, too big for anything else). That they are Swainson's or red-tailed is logical. My quiet hope is that they might be ferruginous hawks. A first look through the binoculars and "none of the above" is the only answer I can come up with.

In Peterson's field guide, small arrows point assuredly to

the two or three characteristics which distinguish each bird. The arrows next to the red-tailed are aimed at the dark belly band and not surprisingly at the bold russet of the tail. For the classic Swainson's, it's a necklace of brown feathers against a creamy breast. The guide thoughtfully provides pages titled "Buteos Overhead," idealized renderings of underwing patterns promising quick and certain identification of birds soaring far above. Peterson's clear, bold illustrations belie a complexity of size and coloring only hinted at in the more cautionary text. The written descriptions are riddled with such confidence-shakers as "might" and "may," "could" and "sometimes." At the best of times, perhaps only half the great hawks match their model field marks. The rest show any number of the wrong signs in the wrong combinations, and the five birds standing quietly in the stubble field have obviously not read Peterson.

Two adults and three young of the year, they are waiting for the sun to generate thermals to soar on, and it is their clear, snow-white breasts which breed the faint promise they might be the elusive ferruginous hawk. They show no hint of a warm brown cowl to mark them as light-phase Swainson's and nothing to suggest the waistcoat banding or rufous tail of the red-tailed. While these are big birds, the adult female properly larger than her mate, they are not as big as ferruginous hawks should be. And they are too close to man, too close to the farm house across the road and standing on the cultivated land which is anathema to their kind.

Sensing the air is right, one after another launches itself from the field and climbs slowly over the river valley, flashing bold white patches on their upper wings that put an end to speculation and wishful thinking. These are Krider's red-tailed, the palest of their infinitely variable kind and the closest any red-tailed comes to being a pure prairie hawk. But any disappointment in fixing their name evaporates in the swooping, circling, soaring magic of pure white against the blue of late morning.

It was these hawks, perched on their roadside fence posts or soaring everywhere above the rolling plains, that gave me back my childhood fascination with the naming of birds. Growing up in England, I had begun learning how to tell one songbird from another and even collected their eggs, keeping the carefully blown shells in shoe boxes padded with cotton batting. But my curiosity did not survive the transatlantic crossing, and it would be twenty-five years before the Swainson's and the red-tailed of my new home in Alberta would send me in search of binoculars and bird books again.

One or another of the twelve North American buteos, the so-called buzzard hawks, occupies nearly every specialized niche on the North American continent. Some, like Harris's hawk, are sedentary, confined to the deserts of the southwest. Others, like the Arctic-breeding rough-legged and the New England red-shouldered, move only as far from their summer grounds as winter cold and the need for food dictate. Swainson's hawk pulls out all the stops to spend the northern winter over the boundless grass of full summer on the Argentine pampas.

Larger than the falcons, harriers and accipiters, bested in size and soaring skill only by the eagles, four great hawks dominate the high plains of the Milk River country: the over-wintering rough-legged, the red-tailed and Swainson's of the transitional margins, and in the pure heart of the shortgrass, the ferruginous hawk.

Early in the morning, before the sun has generated the

thermal currents on which they soar, or during the brief rain-storms which drive their prey to cover, the summer buteos—the red-tailed and the Swainson's—retreat in the hundreds to the fence posts and telephone poles along the roads. These are the flexible, coexistent generalists of the plains, each with its own particularities but each with a reasonable tolerance for change.

The red-tailed is the most complex, a case study in diversi-ty. Ornithologists recognize seven distinct subspecies with one, the dark Harlan's hawk of Alaska, only drawn into the fold within the last two decades. (Such decisions are not without controversy, and within the small, contentious circle of the American Ornithologists Union there is much sympathy for a retrial.) There is some subtle variation of the basic red-tailed model suited to every part of North America. On the Great Plains, the dark-backed eastern red-tailed gives way to a larger, rustier western cousin and to the Krider's, but generalizations about pattern and color are dangerous in any hawk, and the differences within subspecies can take them through almost every gradation from gingered white to dark chocolate.

The red-tailed is the buteo of the parkland forest margins, soaring from its perch high on a cottonwood or telephone pole or dropping like a rock onto the ground squirrels, rabbits and mice, which are its preferred prey. It does not like the agora-phobia-inducing spaces of the true plains, preferring instead to nest in the small woodlots or shelterbelts created by the home-steaders' need to see trees on their skyline.

Those same homesteaders shot them easily off their fence post perches, accepting the truth of their chicken hawk nick-name. While changing attitudes and protective laws (not to mention the disappearance of the family farm with its attendant chicken coop) have stopped the shooting, the poisoning of ground squirrels and grasshoppers has killed far more red-tailed, and every other species of raptor, than any number of farm boys with their .22 rifles.

Swainson's hawk can live with fewer trees. Though there are small eastern populations, this is the common buteo of the southern prairies, one step more specialized than the red-tailed, one step closer to the heart of the shortgrass. It will live with the presence of humans, taking full advantage of planting and harvest days to hunt the displaced voles, mice and larger insects, but it keeps a more respectful distance between itself and the farmyard.

The Swainson's long migration brings it back to the plains later in the spring than the red-tailed, and its young are tied to the nest well into July. Where the red-tailed will only nest high in mature cottonwoods, Swainson's will take what it can get, assembling its flattened mass of twigs in a coulee bottom willow bush, a thicket of thorny buffaloberry or in the overgrown caragana windbreak of an abandoned homeplace.

In August, the shortgrass country is alive with the great hawks. Where there were two in the spring, now there are four or five. Though their young have fully fledged and abandoned the nest, the adults still hold their families together, teaching by example how to hunt insects and small rodents. With the swathers and combines out in the fields, the hunting is as good as it has been since spring planting, and the young learn quickly.

By the end of the month the families have drifted apart, abandoning the nesting territories so fiercely defended through the spring and summer, and begun to wander south. Before the middle of September, the Swainson's will be gone. Individually or in loose-knit groups, they ride the thermals down the eastern slope of the Great Divide, funneling in their thousands through the natural bottlenecks of south Texas and Panama on the overland route to their second summer of the year.

The red-tailed hawks can afford to stay awhile longer. Theirs is not so much a migration as a general retreat. From September until the middle of October, as their prey withdraws underground and the harvests end, they slide away to the south, only as far as the changing weather pushes them, eventually merging with the year-round residents of southern Kansas, Oklahoma and the Texas Panhandle.

Fewer than six weeks from the time of their greatest concentrations, given a cold snap and the first high-ground snows, the last of the buteos are gone from the shortgrass. Their sudden absence is remarkable, a surprise recognition that where they seemed to be everywhere one day, the next they are none. But for the skeins of migrating ducks and geese, the skies are clear and empty, the fence posts and telephone poles occupied only by magpies and the few remaining crows. Then, perhaps only a fortnight after the hawks have gone, a familiar silhouette reappears, soaring high over the ridges and across the pastures. The first of the rough-legged are drifting south from the tundra.

The plains buteos—the red-tails, the Swainson's and the rough-legged—have adapted to man's presence on their plains, overbalancing an "improved" habitat against the predations of rifle and poison, bending their behavior to flourish in the planted windbreaks and feast on the bounty of insects and rodents of the planted land. But there is one among them which still holds the purest essence of what makes their kind, one which is still tied utterly and inflexibly to the pure shortgrass. Where other buteos can venture out into the driest heart of the high plains, there is one that cannot leave it. If any single, living thing best represents the grand contradiction of vast space and fine tolerance which is the Milk River country, it is *Buteo regalis*, the great ferruginous hawk.

The largest and most beautiful of North American buteos, the ferruginous hawk is a near-perfect adaptation to life on the high plains. The price of near perfection, though, is a small allowance for flexibility and, as the shortgrass prairie went under the plow, it pulled *B. regalis* down with it.

In Alberta, *Buteo regalis* is classified as a threatened species, the only one of its family to be so dubiously honored. In the official scheme of things, this puts it one step away from endangered and two shy of extirpated, or regionally extinct. *Threatened* says that a species' future is uncertain unless the specific hazards to its survival are removed or alleviated. For the eagles or the peregrine falcons, such help can be as straightforward as a ban on pesticides or the enforcement of stiff penalties for hunting. For the ferruginous hawk, the problem is not one of specific threats but of the shrinking of the whole shortgrass ecosystem.

At the turn of the century, as the homesteaders pushed into the margins, the ferruginous hawk fell back, steadily retreating into the heart of the drylands. As the number of grass fires decreased, the open prairies were invaded by trees and shrubs, natural hazards in the ferruginous hawk's straight-line pursuit of prey. As the early poisoning campaigns against the ground squirrel increased, the ferruginous's pragmatic willingness to eat carrion and share it with its young probably killed them in substantial numbers. Newer, more sophisticated poisons have affected their ability to reproduce and have occasionally spawned some bizarre mutations. Within forty years of the homestead fever, the ferruginous occupied only half of its previous range, the half that had escaped cultivation. It is certainly lost to the dryland interior of British Columbia and probably already gone from Manitoba. Today, the fewer than two thousand pairs which nest in Alberta represent well over half the Canadian population and approach forty percent of all the ferruginous hawks in existence.

Still, where it survives, it flourishes. Its three to five eggs balance a high infant mortality, and where the young survive their first year they can live for fifteen or even twenty more. Despite constant efforts to eradicate the Richardson's ground squirrel, it is still plentiful, and a breeding pair of ferruginous hawks may take up to five hundred to their nest in a single season. Changing attitudes have reduced the gratuitous shooting, and in some areas artificial nesting platforms have been provided, which ferruginous hawks take readily to. They will live with sheep or open-range cattle, but not with a close human presence and will desert any threatened nest during incubation.

Like everything else on which we have inflicted the words *threatened* or *endangered*, the great hawk has drawn about it a circle of passionate defenders. Scientists and birders, naturalists, schoolchildren and even the occasional rancher or farmer are intent on keeping it from oblivion, fighting to avoid writing the brief epitaph "extirpated" next to its pictures in the books.

With the ferruginous hawk's new celebrity have come reams of careful studies—bibliographies that run to page on page of tightly spaced entries—and detailed statistics. Nesting surveys, bandings and census counts have become incredibly precise, telling us that this year there are just this many more (or less) than there were last year, that this pair has raised this many young this year. These are not estimates, not the kind of educated guesses we make about other, more numerous, species.

It's the same steady slide toward gone that lets us know exactly how many buffalo there are, tells us just where the swift foxes and the burrowing owls are, and lets us count the black-footed ferrets on the fingers of one hand. These are hard numbers and serious truths made possible only because there are so pitifully few of them left.

As it is for all of our bellwether species (and the Milk River country boasts far more than its share), the ferruginous hawk was almost lost even before we knew it was there. And like the swift fox and the burrowing owl, the key to the survival of the ferruginous hawk is clear and simple—as clear and simple as it is impossible. The great hawk needs only that things be the way they used to be. We can help it with nest poles to replace the few aging, cattle-rubbed trees and limit the poisons we use on ground squirrels. We can educate landowners and hope that the new economics of farming mean that no more of the wild country will be put to the plow. But we cannot remove the power lines and roads, nor teach young hawks to avoid speeding cars and trucks. And we cannot bring back the vast oceans of grass over which the ferruginous hawk was meant to soar.

The ferruginous hawk is easy to spot even for a beginning birder. Where it lives, there is nowhere for it to hide. Mistaking the pale Krider's for a ferruginous is understandable, but taking a ferruginous for anything else is impossible. With the much larger females approaching twenty-six inches in length with a wingspan of well over four feet, there is no other summer buteo which approaches it for sheer size. Indeed, it has been suggested that were it an Old World raptor the ferruginous hawk would be classed with the eagles. Like all buteos, the ferruginous comes in a wide range of colors from chocolate to near white, but on the northern plains the pale, reddish brown (hence the name *ferrugo* from the Latin for "rust") form predominates. No other hawk shows its mix of red-brown back, snow-white underside and rust-colored legs which show as a dark V on the belly as it sweeps overhead.

I don't bother to look for the ferruginous hawk where the prairie has been planted to cereal monocultures or where there are copses and windbreaks around a ranch house. These are places it will not tolerate. On their first migrations, the young of the year and the immature may wander briefly through towns like Lethbridge or even Calgary, seeking a breeding territory of their own, but instinct will eventually pull them back to where they were born, back into the wide, dry core.

I look for the ferruginous near a huge ramshackle nest in the only tree for miles around or on the sheltered side of a coulee. Where there is neither tree nor rock, I look in some sheltering hollow on the ground for a rough pile of detritus, a heap of sticks and cow dung and broken fence rail and anything else that can be scrounged from a bare land. Near a ground squirrel colony, I watch for the long, low, terrain-hugging flight of an outsized harrier or for a dark shape crouched beside a burrow, waiting patiently for an over-confident, all-clear whistle to bring the ground squirrels up.

I can look for the ferruginous on the ground or a thousand feet up in a crystal blue sky, but first I must go to the loneliest places, where no one else goes. I walk away from the roads, out to where there is nothing but space, and sometimes there it will be. This great, pale bird is the purest expression of its kind, the living soul of the high plains, and as long as it can hold on here, there is still some hope for this last shortgrass prairie.

It could have been a paradise; maybe it was, maybe it still is.

—WILLIAM KITTREDGE

COMING AROUND AGAIN

Alberta's Highway 880 crosses the Milk on a new bridge, one of only two east of Writing-On-Stone, one of only five along the full length of the stream from the town of Milk River to where it flows back into Montana. Here below the arc of the river is the true heart of the country, and the sense of emptiness and isolation can be almost overwhelming. The flare of the sun's reflection on the steel roofs of distant ranch buildings can be the only sign of a human presence.

At the end of the bridge, a sign points to the Ross Ranches five miles east. The Ross family has been raising cattle somewhere in this country almost from the beginning, and their homeplace is the only one on the south bank of the river for miles in either direction. Here, before the Milk slips into its great canyon, it flows through a smooth, shallow valley lined with low cutbanks and scrub willow.

Though the river is a rich, dark green, the low, wet sandbars which crisscross the main channel say that it is running shallower than it first appears, and the Ross's white-faced cattle can wade across it without difficulty. Perhaps a hundred cows with their calves have been drawn down to its banks on this hot, late-summer afternoon. As it is everywhere across the breadth of this country, the river's visible effect on the land is lost almost at its margin, and the green ends abruptly where the drying grass begins. Breed Creek (still "Half-Breed" on some earlier maps) comes up from Montana in a narrow snake of willow bush, but this late in the year there is no flowing water left in it. A hot, drying wind pours across the whole sweep of the land, strong and constant, through the natural funnel between the Sweetgrass Hills.

The potent mix of need and expectation which drove the settlement of the North American West never rested heavily on the shoulders of the Milk River. The fur traders gave it a wide berth, relying on the Saskatchewan, the Missouri and the Yellowstone to take them to the mountains and up to the divide. Following in the traders' wake, the first settlers westering from the Mississippi rushed across the high plains, bound for California and the Oregon Territory. Within two years of the end of the Civil War, the driving of the last spike in America's transcontinental railroad did not spur development in the center of the continent but served simply to provide a faster, more efficient connection between the East and gold-rich California. The first white settlements on the high plains came in at right angles to the wagon trails and the railways, repopulating the vacuum created by the precipitous decline of the buffalo and the cultures which the great herds had supported.

Within a decade of the end of the Civil War, Texas cattle had swept north from the panhandle across the length and breadth of the high plains, merging along the eastern slope of the Rockies with the herds of western livestock which had paralleled them up from California. From the first great drives up the Chisholm Trail in 1867, the growth of the cattle kingdom was as spectacular as it was unstoppable, and by 1878 the descendants of those raw Texas cows were grazing in the foothills country of the Bow River Valley two hundred miles north of the 49th parallel. Still, it would be years before they came into the Milk River country.

The first cattle ushered in Alberta's short-lived era of free grass and open range. The romantic heyday of the cattle industry, those few years between the arrival of the Mounties and the coming of the Canadian Pacific, saw the birth of a Canadian ranching aristocracy. Largely confined to the narrow strip of rich grassland between Calgary and the border, the great ranches may have been stocked with American cattle and watched over by American cowboys, but the ranch owners themselves were overwhelmingly Canadian or British. They were retired veterans of the Mounted Police, the landless sons of England's landed gentry or eastern entrepreneurs with a clear sense of what the coming of the railway would mean to the West.

Until the CPR reached the foothills in the summer of 1883, the market for Alberta beef had been largely the Mounted Police forts and the small communities which were growing up around them, the Treaty Seven reserves and the CPR road builders. The railway opened Chicago and Toronto and the East Coast ports to Alberta cattle; it opened Alberta to the national dream, and hard on the heels of the navvies, the chainmen of the Dominion Land Survey drew their base lines and meridians onto the trackless prairie. The division of the West into townships and sections spelled the end of the open range.

To the politicians and mandarins of the federal government, the ultimate absentee landlords, the Great Plains were wasted on cattle. At first they encouraged the stockmen. After all, any profitable use of the land was preferable to leaving it in its natural state, and besides they had made commitments to provide beef to the newly settled Indians. Their final vision, though, was still tied to the old Jeffersonian notions of small family farms spread evenly across the land, as they did in Europe and along the eastern seaboard. The vision had already taken root in the rich bottomlands of Manitoba's Red River, and there was no reason for them to suppose it would not survive all the way to the Rockies.

For the railway, cattle were an important cargo, but they were a one-way cargo, not valuable enough to recover the huge cost of building and operating the line. In return for stitching the country together, the Canadian Pacific had negotiated title to a staggering twenty-five million acres of western land. It was a deal that only made sense if that land was carved into homesteads populated by families who bought their tickets west from the same railway and eventually used its rolling stock to send their produce east. It was a vision which fit perfectly with Ottawa's.

With the surveys came the leases, and with the leases came the barbed wire. From the early 1880s, the cattlemen would graze their livestock only at the pleasure of their federal landlords, who would give no assurance beyond five or ten years that the leases would be renewed. The cattle industry flourished through that first post-railway decade, but it was living on borrowed time. Pressure from homesteaders had begun to build almost before the CPR had pushed tracks up to the divide, and it peaked at the beginning of the 1890s. Everywhere there was easy water and day-haul access to the railway, squatters began to assert their rights to the public lands on which the great ranchers raised their cattle. To the south, below the old ranching capital of Fort Macleod, the first wave of Mormon settlers had begun the work of digging irrigation canals and turning the grass under. Their eyes were on raising crops, not grazing cattle.

Slowly at first, the cattlemen's access to the better lands was blocked. The ranchers responded by purchasing more, but they could only pay for so much. When the prime lands had been taken up, the pressure from the homestead movement, aided by growing political clout and an increasingly sympathetic government, expanded outward toward the drier, rougher country. The new Calgary and Edmonton railway, running south toward Fort Macleod and Lethbridge, had opened the lands along the old Whoop-Up and Calgary trails, and fields of wheat soon separated the foothills cattle from their old flatland ranges to the east. As the century turned, the preeminence of the great western ranches was all but finished.

To the south and east, deep in the Milk River border country, the pattern of ranch development did not follow the foothills model. Politics and practicalities had brought the CPR main line into Alberta along the South rather than the North Saskatchewan River, but west of Medicine Hat it veered north and west toward Calgary rather than the Crowsnest Pass via the heart of Palliser's Triangle. Still dogged by its desert reputation, the area held little attraction for the boosters or homesteaders, and for years after the boundary survey and the Mounties' long march, the land below the Cypress Hills remained the province of the Metis, the wolfers and the whiskey traders.

Below the 49th, with the buffalo gone and the "Indian trouble" all but settled by the late 1870s, beef cattle swept onto the northern tier. So powerful was the attraction of this last free grass that by the middle of the 1880s Montana's Milk River ranges were hopelessly overcrowded and badly overgrazed. With only small markers every three miles or so to signal the border, it was inevitable that Montana cattle spilled across the line and onto the largely unpopulated Canadian grass.

In 1886 the Canadian government was forced to restrict American access to its southern rangelands. Stiff tariffs were imposed on the importation of American stock, and in at least one case, "straying" American cattle were seized and sold by the Mounted Police. With the closing of the free range in Montana and the imposition of tariffs, quarantines and branding requirements along the border, the American outfits moved to legitimize their presence above the border. The Spencer Brothers brought their 3CU brand to the banks of the Milk River in 1897, followed by the birth of the P-Cross, the Q and the Cross Z in the coulees and canyons of the Lost River, Sage and Manyberries creeks. When, in 1902, U.S. ranchers and their cattle were finally allowed access to Canadian leases, hundreds of thousands of acres between the border and the Cypress Hills were paid for in American dollars, ensuring that the American influence in Milk River country remained dominant.

The Americans joined those few English and Canadian ranchers who had already established operations south of Medicine Hat. Englishman Sydney Hooper is said to have been the first into the country, settling along Manyberries Creek in the mid-1880s on what was then called the Fiddle Back Ranch. Others came from east and west, from Saskatchewan's Maple Creek district and from the foothills between Calgary and Fort Macleod. If the land was not as productive, it was a good deal cheaper, and without a railway there was little or no pressure from the sodbusters.

The open range survived in Milk River country longer than anywhere else, but it could not last. Eventually, inevitably, the pressures of the homestead movement began to push in, and the boom-and-bust story which had already been told across the central prairies from Winnipeg to the foothills was to be repeated.

Twin River, named for the confluence of the North and South forks of the Milk, was the first provincial grazing reserve, a direct, heart-of-the-Depression attempt to staunch the flood of worn-out homesteaders and small scale ranchers, who threatened to leave the land an empty, burned-out shell. As the drought and depression of the post-war twenties deepened and the tiny homesteads began to blow away, diversification became the rallying cry of the dryland boosters. Lacking the acreage to run sufficient numbers of cattle and facing failure after failure of the wheat crops, the small landowner was encouraged to look back at the old eastern models, to plant some wheat, keep some livestock and expand the small vegetable patch. When the wheat dried up, there would be an income from cream or eggs. When the rains came and the grains flourished, the extra money would allow for expansion or modernization or paying off debts. In theory, it was a sound solution. In practice, it made matters worse. Diversification meant more demands on a land which was already overtaxed. Expansion required more feed, more water and more investment; and when the rains failed, the diversified dryland farmer found himself with more mouths to feed and more crops to water. A man who could not feed his family could not feed his cattle or his hogs or even his chickens.

Diversification was the answer, but not on the quaint scale imagined. It was the ranchers who had the solution. The best of them, those who had been in for the long haul, had learned quickly the limits of the land. In their resistance to the homesteaders, they had been taken for arrogant, aristocratic and even unpatriotic (and many may have been), but they knew something the boosters did not know or did not want to know. They knew that in this country, land—lots of land—was everything.

In the driest heart of the Milk River country, on land where one homestead-sized parcel might be sufficient to sustain only two or perhaps three head of cattle in a good year, few could hope to own enough natural grass to survive in the livestock business. Where there were bottomlands watered by spring flooding, they fenced meadows and raised hay and feed grains. In a land of coulees and potholes, they dammed and diked the small creeks to water their stock in the parched midsummer. They moved their cattle around the country, grazing here in the spring and there in the summer, keeping them away from certain places at certain times of the year, knowing the grazing would change with the seasons. And knowing the wideopen range was gone forever, they began to share what was left.

It was an idea which had been floated along the lower Milk when that country was first opened—keeping a township-wide strip of native grass between the irrigated valley and the upland homesteads—but it was too reasonable to stand up to the terrible thirst for land at any cost. It was an idea which eventually put down its first firm roots in Montana's Powder River country on the dry, wide-open southeastern ranges, which showed the classic twenties mix of overgrazed pasture and abandoned homesteads. The Mizpah-Pumpkin Grazing Association was the first attempt at cooperative, professional range management, the first concerted effort to undo the excesses of the past decades for which both rancher and sodbuster were responsible.

In 1935, seven years after the Mizpah experiment began, the Alberta government opened the Twin River Range.

The principles of the plan are simple and obvious: graze cattle on cooperative grass through the summer while the homeplace is given over to the raising of hay, alfalfa or feed grains. Bring the cows home in the fall and feed them that hay and grain through the winter and the calving season. Sell the yearlings in the spring, and put the cows with their new calves back on the summer range, which has had time to recover from the previous season's grazing. It's public land with private management, and it seems to have been working well for the past sixty years.

From mid-May until well into October, the great provincial grazing reserves—Twin River, Sage Creek and Pinhorn—are stocked with the cows and calves of what are called the patrons, the member ranchers and farmers without sufficient land or leases to sustain a self-contained cattle operation. The reserves are home to herds of cooperatively owned bulls, too. The associations, the supervisors and the provincial government know what the range can support, and the numbers of animals turned onto the native grass pastures will change from year to year according to the conditions. It's all about something called the AUM—the Animal Unit Month—and in principle it is the only sensible way to make the most of the what the land will allow.

One AUM is what one mature cow with her calf can eat in a month, and it's the number of AUMs that determines both what will be brought onto the range and how much each rancher will pay. It's the best system, but not a perfect system. The long-term trend in the cattle business has been toward bigger animals to carry more weight to market in the same short period of time. With larger cows carrying larger calves and steady improvements to early season feeding programs, calves just turned out onto the reserves are carrying perhaps fifty percent more weight than they might have a few short decades back. The managers have the right to determine what constitutes an AUM and adjust their permits accordingly, but it's a rare rancher who is willing to see his access to the grass limited. The problem of outsized beef, however, may soon be moot, resolved by the changing tastes of the consumer.

The cattle business has always been simpler and more straightforward than the growing of grain. It has never lived on the impossible complexities of subsidy and marketing board, never been faced with the need for two hundred thousand dollars worth of tractor, massive irrigation systems or endless supplies of high-priced insecticides, herbicides and the latest in miracle fertilizers. It has been simpler for the cattleman because cattle belong here on these dry grasslands in a way wheat and barley and canola never have. But the price of that simplicity, the cost of living without the protective blanket of price-support structures and national policies, has been a life lived closer to the edge. The simple realities of supply and demand, of changing tastes and uncertain weather, have always worked against the cattleman with an unrelenting certainty.

With a fair-sized, debt-free spread, two hundred head will make a good living for a family willing to do the work. More cattle might mean more protection from the constant rise and fall of the market, but more cattle means more land, and land is expensive. So is the cost of the money it takes to buy it. The provincial reserves and the cooperative pastures have made it possible for the smaller operator to stay in the business, avoiding the mass consolidations and huge, monolithic operations that are norm for the modern Milk River wheat producer. But not all the small operators can get their stock onto a reserve, and a late spring can see a rancher hand-feeding his cattle high-priced fodder well past the time they should be grazing on new grass. A small slip in the price per pound and all that expensive feed can go to make nothing more than a large hole in a small checking account.

It has been that way since the first cows came north across the line. But once again, change is coming to the Milk River country as surely as everywhere across the Canadian West. This time, the new realities may bury once and for all the old animosities between the rancher and the farmer. This time they may have no choice.

Cattle have always left this country on the hoof, carrying only what weight the range grass and winterfeed have given them. They go off to the auction houses in places like Lethbridge to be knocked down as raw material for the feedlots and the slaughter houses, everyone taking his piece of the action, adding his price to the cost the consumer will pay. Part of the reason the cattleman sees so little of the "value-added benefit" (the newest buzzwords in agriculture) that attaches to his cows by the time they get to the table is historical: a bred-in-the-bone mistrust of an uncertain future, the attraction of a dollar now against the hope for two later on. Part of the reason is the high cost of feed.

Across the fence line from the summer grazing cattle, the huge fields of grain come up, ripening from rich green to gold in synchrony with the mellowing of the natural grasses. As the wheat is harvested and pours into the elevators, the cattle pastures have given up what strength they have and begun to dry back toward winter. The perfect solution should be to replace the fading grass with unlimited winter forage, keeping the feed-lots supplied with rich, finishing feed. Until now, that has not been the case. The grain in the fields, from the time it was seed, has been bound for somewhere else. It comes up out of the ground already locked into a welter of price supports and transportation subsidies, designer wheat for the export trade, headed to China and Russia and anywhere else they cannot grow enough to feed themselves. The only way this stuff will end up as meat protein is if the rancher can match the asking price, in effect compete with China and his own federal govern-ment. Or he can pray for a minor disaster, a cold spring or an early fall blizzard, to downgrade the crop and render it fit only for cattle feed.

But the times are right for all this to change. The subsidies are disappearing, and the farmer, like everyone else in a society increasingly obsessed with waving the banner of self-reliance, is facing the realities of supply and demand, of paying the real cost to ship his high-volume, low-value crop halfway around the world. More and more, keeping livestock and growing feed grain are beginning to look like the way to go.

For one thing, beef has once again achieved an air of respectability with the consumer. Gone are the cholesterol-rid-den, hormone-packed time bombs guaranteed to bring on heart attacks, and in their place is a variety of designer cuts, perfect for the fashionable, low-fat lifestyle. There's less call for platter-sized T-bones and "man-sized" prime-rib dinners, more interest in the perfect six- or even four-ounce steak, more demand for quality over quantity. This will bring smaller cows back into fashion. There will be fewer of the huge Simmental and more of the compact Angus, the leaner, more efficient converters which make more meat on less feed. In the new economics, three calves at five-hundred pounds apiece make more high-priced cuts than two at seven-fifty.

Slowly but surely, the old cycle is coming around again, and the Milk River country is going back toward grass though hopes for the rebirth of the great shortgrass ocean will be disappointed. Dreams of a return to the open range and the old ways will remain just that. They are gone forever. Where the rain and the land is right for it, there will still be huge fields of wheat and barley, increasingly interspersed with canola and mustard and the other specialty crops of the new agriculture. And there will be more alfalfa and other forage crops, grown for winterfeed or to supply the local feedlots, which the new realities should encourage. Perhaps there are dreams of abattoirs, too, and trucks leaving this country filled with beef in high-value packages, not bawling on the hoof.

All this should have a familiar ring to it. It has all been suggested before, back in the twenties, when the first boom was going bust. Diversify, the professors and scientists at Onefour said. Forget all the fantasies. Work with this land and it will yield a living. Perhaps this time we're ready to listen.

*For ten million years they moved like that, until
Europeans came and said that all of it had to belong
to someone.*
—DAN O'BRIEN

ONEFOUR & CATTALO

T here are still buffalo along the Milk River. Though
they are long gone from the open grass of the Sage
Creek and Pinhorn ranges, there are more here now
than at any time since before the turn of the century. As I drive
through the country, it's easy to tell where they are, even when
their humpbacked, chocolate-brown silhouettes are not visible
from the road. There are buffalo wherever the traditional three
or four strands of barbed wire change abruptly to what's called
game fence, a heavy, rectangular steel mesh strung six feet high
or more along a line of supports bearing more resemblance to
telephone poles than fence posts. At nearly a dollar a foot for
the wire alone, it's not the kind of construction used for
domesticated livestock. The ranchers willing to make such a
huge investment need more than nostalgia for a bygone era to
motivate them. They're into buffalo for the money.

   If any single creature has come to symbolize the end of the
Old West—the triumph of profligacy, indifference and sheer

stupidity—it is the buffalo. Still represented everywhere across the West on state and provincial flags and seals, in the center of the Mounties' coat of arms, in painting and pottery, in the names of towns and sports teams, the American bison remains the great unifying symbol for the Great Plains. In its passing it has engendered more sympathy and hand-wringing *mea culpa*s than the simultaneous death of the great nations whose existence the buffalo made possible. The hundreds of books and thousands of articles are awash in almost unbelievable statistics, and every schoolchild can recite some horrible fact about how many buffalo there were and how quickly they died. Still, no matter how impossible the numbers may seem, they all have a ring of truth. When it comes to the buffalo, it is hard to be apocryphal.

It is hard, too, to conjure any real connection between some small, benign pattern of pastured livestock viewed through the mesh of a game fence and the broad, windswept horizons of a place like the Pinhorn. On one hand are these living relics of a lost time; on the other, a fragment of the land which bred them in their millions. I try to put the two together, try to take this twenty or thirty head, multiply them ten-thousand-fold, and imagine them out on the vacant grass, a bawling, drifting carpet of living flesh and dust. To conceive what that must have looked like from the crest of the Milk River Ridge or the Cypress Hills requires an act of pure imagination, a willing suspension of disbelief on a scale few can manage.

How the endless herds swirled around the center of the continent, where they went and how many there really were will never be known, but sense suggests that at least two and perhaps as many as four great herds circled independently through the Milk River country in the course of their constant migration. From their wintering grounds in the western foothills and low mountain valleys, they would shamble out onto the flat-lands following the freshening spring grass. Along the way, the cows dropped their single calves into a world of plenty which would support their rapid growth. Others that had sought shelter in the boreal forest margins would come south to meet them, seeking the same clean grazing lands and the same warming sun. By the time they arrived in the heart of the country, the high summer of the rutting season, the grasses had finished their explosive growth, matured and begun to set their seeds. Another vast herd, perhaps the largest of them all, would have wintered to the south, where cold and snow were less extreme. As the weather moderated, they would have left their worn-out ranges and drifted, like birds on their broad flyways, toward the cooler temperatures and fresh grazing of the northern tier.

Every element in this continental mechanism was locked perfectly in its place; every factor in the grand equation added up to a perfect, dynamic balance. Nowhere else on this planet's dry land did the forces of action and reaction, of co-dependent evolution, conspire to produce such a massive display of flesh and bone. Nothing else on this continent came within a ton of a full-grown buffalo bull; nothing but the birds matched it in its ceaseless wanderings. The infinite grasslands made the buffalo possible, and over the millennia they in turn came to depend on the great herds for their very survival. The buffalo could chew and digest the coarse, tough stuff, take from it what they needed and dump the rest as raw fertilizer back onto the nutrient-thin prairie soil.

For all the spectacular weight of waving grass that the Great Plains displayed, like an iceberg it was only perhaps one tenth of what was really there. Grasses do their work underground, storing up the power to survive in their dense tangle of roots. When grasses grow, they grow not from their tips like trees, but from their base, pushing up new stems to generate their food and set their seeds. With all their power sheltered beneath the ground, they are immune to the extremes of prairie weather, to the flash fires and the great animals which feed on them. It is not simply that the grasses can tolerate such predation, they require it. Where grasslands are not grazed and reprocessed, they will choke and die on their own detritus.

For the buffalo, the need to move was absolute, and the great circles, the relentless motion, would keep the herds on new pastures, allowing the grasses at least a full three seasons of renewal before they were subjected again to the incredible assault of teeth and hooves. In the patterns of their movement, the buffalo were like everything else in this land: flexible and adaptable within a carefully defined set of limitations. Where an area had been particularly hard hit by heavy grazing or drought or fire, the herds would bend around it, not returning for perhaps a decade until it could once again withstand their brief, intense devastation.

The buffalo relied on sheer numbers to counter the deadly perils and natural catastrophes which must have killed them in their thousands. There was the steady predation of the wolf and the grizzly, culling the sick and the old, the slow and the newborn. There were the plains nations with their sophisticated understanding of migration routes and animal behavior, exploiting that life-or-death understanding to provoke a mass stampede over a bluff or stalk quietly around the margins of the herd, taking single animals. The horse and the gun increased their ability to kill the plains buffalo, but until they, too, joined in the last, great slaughter, the herds could easily replace what the hunters took.

Their skeletons and skulls still erode out of coulees and riverbanks everywhere in the Milk River country. The ranchers and hikers who find them look up toward the rim of the cutbanks and wonder about buffalo jumps on the scale of Alberta's Head-Smashed-In or Wyoming's Hell's Half Acre, but it is more likely to have been the rivers themselves that claimed these beasts. Native lore and a hundred firsthand journal accounts tell the story of huge catastrophes. As the great herds swept out on their spring migrations, the buffalo drowned by the thousands in the swollen streams. Ice bridges weakened by the rising water would collapse under their immense weight, stranding bull and cow and calf alike on fractured, fast-moving floes. Herd leaders would lose their footing on sodden, crumbling banks or stumble into quicksand and be washed away. Still tied to their leaders, the rest would follow blindly, and their carcasses would foul the rivers for miles downstream. The beasts died in prairie fires, wind-driven infernos that could sweep across the grasslands faster than they could run, and despite their heavy coats, the worst of the winter blizzards would freeze them solid where they stood. Still, the calving season would replace in a year or two the worst of Nature's toll, leaving the herd even stronger and healthier.

For thousands upon thousands of years, the buffalo were masters of the subtle but absolute terms dictated by the great grasslands, but nothing, not even something so massive and so numerous as the plains bison, could survive what was done to the heart of the continent by white settlement in the space of just a few brief decades at the close of the nineteenth century.

Had the perfect equation changed more slowly, of its own necessity, something of the buffalo would have survived. After all, it had been the slow, steady evolution of thousands of years that had made them possible in the first place. After all, there were the wood buffalo, adapted to live hundreds of miles from the plains in the forests and swamp grasses of far northern Alberta and Saskatchewan. If a wetter, warmer environment had slowly finished off the grasslands, if another continental glacier had come down onto the country, the plains buffalo would have evolved to meet those changes. Given millennia, or even centuries, there would have been descendants living on whatever the ancient grasslands had become.

The buffalo was lost even before serious science could take its measure. In 1886, Washington's National Museum came to the stunned realization that its collections contained not a single decent specimen of the plains buffalo. Chief taxidermist William Hornaday went west to obtain enough prime skins for a great, nostalgic diorama. For the entire month of May, he systematically traveled the country around Miles City, Montana, only to return to Washington empty-handed. The few buffalo he did manage to find were small and unimpressive, ragged and threadbare in their thinning spring coats. He went back again in September, looking for the full, rich robes of autumn. Where only a few years before a good hunter could stand and shoot buffalo until the barrel of his rifle bent from the heat, it took Hornaday eight weeks to down only twenty-five suitable animals. A year later, his competitor from the Museum of Natural History set out for the same country with the same goal and couldn't find a single buffalo. They were perhaps only three or four years too late.

The horror stories of slaughter by railway meat hunters, by sporting European nobility, hide men and, near the end, even by the Indians themselves, are pure grist for the mill of western legend, but all that was almost after the fact, a bloody, spectacular mopping-up operation. The plow and the fence had already finished the buffalo. They were gone from their ranges east of Mississippi by the beginning of the 1830s, and when the first homestead wave broke into Kansas and Nebraska, it washed the buffalo ahead of it, driving a wedge of wheat and wire between the northern and southern herds. As the railways pushed toward the mountains, their work crews lived on the buffalo, and the settlements they spawned along their lines of steel blocked and broke the buffalo's ancient migratory trails.

When the robes had been stripped from the last of the heartland herds, the hunters turned south toward Texas and Oklahoma. It took no more than four years for the high-volume business of killing buffalo to flourish, stall and die, cleansing the panhandle in advance of its next tenants. The rich grass of the southern plains would lie fallow only a year or two before the cattle and plow could put it to a more profitable use.

With the rest of the Great Plains tamed and turned to the purposes of the settler, the civilizing machinery of the new age was finally brought to bear on the upper Missouri, on the last wild place. The pattern of its coming was the same witnessed in Kansas and Texas: the cavalry to break the Indians and the hunters to kill the buffalo followed by the railways, the cattlemen and the homesteaders to make it all into something new.

It may well have been from the summits of places like the Sweetgrass Hills or the Bears Paw Mountains that the great spectacle of the wild buffalo was last witnessed, for it was the herds of northern Montana—of the lower Yellowstone, the Missouri and the Milk—which were the last to go under the gun. The buffalo's ancient need to move brought the last ragged, remnant herds north in the summer of 1883. In that year, railwaymen saw eighty thousand or more cross the Yellowstone near Miles City, headed toward Canada, toward the unbroken chain of killing camps strung along the upper Missouri. Nature drove the buffalo north, the waiting hunters slaughtered them, and the last of wild American bison were gone forever.

The game fences around the buffalo ranches in the Milk River country are high and strong, designed, their keepers say, to prevent the small herds from wandering off. It's a wonderfully innocuous phrase for what a buffalo, free of its fence, would do. Horses and cattle wander, grazing away for a mile or so, blissfully unaware of how far they have gone. Buffalo do not wander and they do not consider any place to be home. Buffalo move. At a steady, plodding walk of five miles per hour, they can be found the next morning miles from a break in their fence, tramping through crops and walking through barbed wire as if it wasn't there. At a run, they can maintain a ground-eating pace of more than twice that speed for ten miles at a stretch. Spooked, they can sprint at better than thirty-five, faster than anything but a pronghorn or a good horse. Valuable now as individual animals, each one an ear-tagged, inoculated singularity, they are rarely allowed to get too far away before being driven back to their tiny, wire-framed pastures or shot before they can inflict too much damage on a neighbor's property.

Remarkably, generations of nothing but fences and virtual hand-feeding do not seem to have changed the buffalo much. They are still as dangerous and intractable as Nature made them, still to be approached only with an excess of caution. How long did it take before the horse and the cow and the sheep lost their urge to wander and were content to stay with the herdsman? Certainly more than the hundred years it has been since the buffalo's last grand progress around the heart of the continent. It would be instructive to see if the ancient urge to move is still intact. Was it learned from the herd or hard-wired into the brain? One suspects it is still there, constrained only by the fences. Surely something in us needs to believe it is, to believe that left to its own devices the buffalo would prove it has not yet lost its inheritance.

We killed them in their millions, this single wild obstacle to the efficient conversion of the West into bite-sized parcels where wheat would grow and quiet, almost housebroken cattle would graze. In those last few years, we put their hides and hair and bones to every kind of purpose, but all the uses we found were by-products of our need to kill them.

Still, there were those who saw in the buffalo something other than a stunning spectacle or a brute impediment to a new world. They were the first to recognize the maze of fine cracks in the perfect vision of the New West. The farther that vision was carried beyond the 100th meridian and the closer it came to the heart of Palliser's Triangle, the wider the cracks grew. The mild, wet years which had brought the first bumper crops of wheat and rich grazing for the cattle evaporated under the hot sun or froze solid in a succession of cold winters. In the decade following World War I, as the droughts deepened and the homesteaders began their exodus, the government started to take stock of the triangle, began for the first time to examine the true nature of the place and what it would support.

Deep in the eastern Alberta border country, between the crossing at Wild Horse and the place where the Milk River slides back into Montana, the square, white-painted buildings and fences of Onefour, the old Dominion Range Experimental Farm, are tangible evidence of a long-term attempt to forge a workable compromise between the need to use this land and the absolute limitations it imposes. That the farm—a charming misnomer for a tract of better than eighteen thousand acres—was built here in the driest, loneliest part of the country is a sign of the seriousness of the place. There had always been lots of advice available, solutions suggested from the hothouse laboratories of eastern universities or pulled out of thin air by land agent boosters, but this was an effort to put all the theories to the test in the very place where they would have to work. It also put the money and power of the federal government to work among the people who knew the land best.

Onefour came upon me as a complete surprise as I drove around a graveled curve on Highway 502 perhaps fifteen miles east from Highway 41. Were this road south of the border, I might have assumed it to be some vestige of the Cold War, something to do with the Minuteman missile silos which once strung along the entire length of the border between the Dakotas and the Great Divide. Second thoughts might have wanted to make it into one of the huge Hutterite colonies which dot this country. It has the right austere, industrial look about it. Even the name has a practical ring: Onefour, coined from its location in Township One, Range Four.

Onefour is the perfect location for learning the realities of life in the drylands. One can only be impressed by the dedication of the scientists and range managers who moved out here to the middle of nowhere and lived crudely in borrowed buildings while they tried to save this place and its people. There were more people living here when the range station was built in 1927, but even before the clearances it was never what you could call crowded. Today, anything but farm equipment on these roads is a rarity. This is still a place so lonely that I once came upon a pronghorn antelope resting unconcerned on the

warm gravel in the middle of the road. Roused but not particularly alarmed by my truck, she paced off along the gravel at an
effortless thirty miles an hour until she veered off to one side,
flattened herself under the bottom strand of the barbed-wire
fence and emerged on the other side with nothing more than an
indifferent glance back at her pursuer.

Just west of Onefour, Lost River cuts across the road in a
multicolored sandstone confusion of hoodoos and side draws.
Prairie falcons and golden eagles sweep back and forth between
their nests and the flatlands above the far rim of the canyon.
But for the occasional year when the spring runoff is high, this
is a river in name only. A pale mist of green along the bottom
of the valley is the only sign that there may be water here,
buried deep under the sand and loose stones. I walk a half-mile
up the Lost River, and all the stories about the Mounties' near-
fatal introduction to the heart of the West begin to take on a
chilling reality. In the shimmering heat of late July, just looking
at this place brings on a fierce thirst. In summer, it would make
a travel poster for the Arizona desert, and what it would be like
in a forty-below January blizzard doesn't bear thinking about. It
doesn't look much like buffalo country—camels would be a
more obvious choice—and it's miles from anything that could
put meat on a Hereford steer.

The work the scientists did here through the most desperate
years of the Great Depression made a difference, and without
them this country might well have slid the last short stretch back
to the near-desert it had always wanted to be. At Onefour and
other experimental stations in the drylands of Saskatchewan,
they discovered, developed and tirelessly promoted the merits
of crested wheatgrass as the salvation for overgrazed pastures
and drought-blown soil. They pushed the idea of communal

grazing preserves and searched for the best way to build dugouts and dikes to water the livestock and irrigate the spring hay meadows. They learned from those who had managed to survive in this place and from those who had lost and left. And they studied the buffalo.

Though the ranchers of the eastern Milk River had adapted as best they knew how to the limitations of the shortgrass prairie, they still carried some of the deep instincts born in the richer pastures of the East or the foothills. They let their herds fend for themselves on summer grass while they worked their hay meadows and their winter ranges, building up feed to carry their cattle through six months and more until the native grasses greened again. They tried to build a steady growth toward market size, tried not to lose the precious weight gains of summer in the cold of December, but the cost of hand-rearing cattle through more than half a year could be more than the meat was worth. How, they wondered at Onefour, did the buffalo flourish on the frozen ground of a western winter?

It was at Onefour that speculation and aphorism were put to the hard test of field experiments. Buffalo lived through the winter by borrowing on the flesh and fat of their summer grazing, losing mass in the process, but managing to find enough feed to stave off starvation. Domestic cattle could do the same. "Well summered and half wintered" went the old adage, and at Onefour they proved its truth. Lighter rations through the winter might cost a steer three hundred pounds, but the healthy animal feeding on the new spring grass would easily put that and more back on, emerging ready for market at the same time and the same weight as those kept on a heavy diet of high-priced winterfeed.

But the Dominion Range Experimental Farm did not

become famous for simply musing about the buffalo's perfect adaptation to the shortgrass plains. Onefour is best known not for its huge successes but for one near-success: the great cattalo experiment.

Speculation about crossing the buffalo with the domestic cow had been around since the earliest days of the Spanish settlements. There were small herds of the hybrids along the eastern seaboard before the American Revolution, but they remained more a curiosity than a serious threat to the purebred European cattle. Interest in the merits of a buffalo cross grew again as encroaching settlements tested the limits of domestic cattle to survive in the driest, coldest parts of the continent. It was the ability of such marginal places to support the buffalo in their hundreds of thousands which had first convinced the newcomers that the land must, despite appearances, be wonderfully fertile. In places it was, but there were millions of acres which could take the measure of even the hardiest domestic breed.

What the scientists were after at Onefour was the same combination of traits they had first tried to mix in 1915 using the government buffalo herd at Wainwright. They were out to create something which could produce the high quality meat of domestic beef cattle from an animal with the buffalo's ability to survive the brutal privations of the western winter. It was axiomatic that the buffalo would not have died in their thousands as their domestic cousins did during the legendary killing cold and snow of 1906 and 1907.

The buffalo bull—domestic cow cross often proved fatal to both mother and calf. The reverse seemed to solve the mortality problem, but getting an otherwise efficient domestic bull to go anywhere near a buffalo cow was a challenge in itself. The natural roadblock to hybridization—sterile offspring—was true only of the male progeny, and back-breeding the females to either pure species seemed to improve fertility. Successions of backcrossing led eventually to a beast somewhere around fifteen percent pure buffalo, a ratio that seemed to blend the most desirable characteristics. These cattalo were certainly winter hardy, prepared to continue rummaging through the snow to feed in the most appalling conditions. They inherited something of the buffalo's thick, woolly coat, too, which no doubt contributed to their cold weather staying power. Still, cattalo never really got off the drawing board.

If a camel is a horse designed by a committee, then the cattalo was proof that compromise is not always the road to perfection. It was fertile enough, but could not match the reliability of domestic cattle. The reason may have been Nature's resistance to hybrids or a remnant of the buffalo's congenitally lower birthrate. It was a good deal more tractable than the buffalo, and it could put on weight quickly enough, efficiently converting a coarser kind of feed, thriving on poorer range, but the meat it produced never quite equaled the standards of the domestic breeds. The vestigial hump, which gave it an odd, front-heavy profile, made it light in the rear, the place where the serious money beef was supposed to be.

The cattalo experiments were finally abandoned in 1964, and the herd was destroyed. In the end, it became unprofitable to continue such long-term fine tuning. There were pure domestic crosses which were proving more than winter hardy enough, and careful management of the cooperative ranges made winterfeeding a less onerous task. Changing times meant the cattalo just wasn't worth the candle, but those same times have refocused attention on the real thing.

In times obsessed with feeling and fashion, buffalo has

become the perfect designer meat. Usually sold through specialty shops with assurances of being drug-free, it is reckoned to be low in cholesterol. Advertising promotes its richer, gamey taste and its tender, juicy texture. It is popular with tourist restaurants across the West, and in the summer the buffalo burger is everywhere. Those who are willing to make an investment in buffalo ranching find there is a call for all they can produce, and its substantially higher cost will keep it from hurting the market for their neighbor's beef. Once again, there is a demand for the robes and hides, and the skulls which once went east by the trainload for fertilizer can easily fetch four hundred dollars in trendy western furnishing shops.

South of the border, the buffalo has acquired a definite cachet among the big-money recreational ranchers—the media stars and corporate executives—who have begun to populate places like the Yellowstone Valley around Big Timber and Livingston. For part-time residents who don't need their land to produce a living, a herd of buffalo is a symbolic commitment to preserving something of the great grasslands as they were before the assault of the cattlemen and the homesteaders, and keeping buffalo can be an expensive fantasy, even for those whose herds are in demand now that the western movie is once again fashionable.

And there are the more than two thousand head which still roam Yellowstone National Park. The last so-called free-range herd in America, they are as much a part of the tourists' western experience as the geysers and the grizzly bears. All in all, the sight of the Yellowstone herd conveys an authentic sense of what the buffalo used to be, and the reaction to seeing them for the first time is invariably the same: amazement and elation fast tempered by a sad, quiet ache. To see them now is to know instinctively what they must once have been and to know, too, that but for this small herd they will never again be seen ranging freely on the high plains.

The buffalo remains the one great symbol of what was lost when the vast shortgrass plains went under the surveyor's transit and the moldboard plow. So massive in size and huge in number were the buffalo—what some ecologists like to call charismatic megafauna—that their catastrophic collapse has overshadowed all the other living things that went down with them. On the grim lists of species identified as being at risk, threatened, endangered or extirpated, the plants and animals of the shortgrass figure disproportionately large in both number and variety. They are a testament to how tightly the various threads of life are woven in the shortgrass.

Just as the shortgrass was tied to the narrow range of climatic conditions to which it was perfectly evolved, so the animals which lived here were tied to the grass and to one another. They were left undisturbed longer than anywhere else on the Great Plains, but when the animals of this last place finally faced the plow and the poisons, there was nowhere else for them to go. The prairie dog, the black-footed ferret, the swift fox, the burrowing owl, the prairie chicken, the ferruginous hawk—the list goes on, and trying to hybridize some new form of these pure plains creatures to withstand the changes that have been brought down upon them will not work any better than it did with the cattalo.

Our attitude toward these smaller, less obviously spectacular creatures is the old mix of active predation and passionate defense larded with wide bands of indifference. There are still plenty of farmers and ranchers who see the networks of ground squirrel tunnels as something which devalues their land, costs them bushels per acre and interferes with their grazing cattle and horses. But in their attacks on the ground squirrels, the ranchers and farmers also attack the creatures that rely on the ground squirrels and their burrow towns.

It's odd that among all the threatened or extirpated species of the plains, almost no one is talking about the prairie dog. It was wiped out decades ago, and its demise brought about the first precipitous declines in the numbers of most of the animals which now grace our endangered species lists. The swift foxes and burrowing owls lived in the prairie dog's abandoned holes. The ferrets lived in their burrows, too, and hunted them through the huge networks of interconnected tunnels. Above ground, the ferruginous hawk would nest close to the towns and feed its young almost exclusively on prairie dogs. But the prairie dog will remain on Alberta's extirpated list, and there are many who would like to see it joined by the ground squirrel. In the eyes of nearly everyone, the prairie dog is still the ultimate pest, and suggesting its reintroduction would be about as popular with ranchers and farmers as proposing the return of the plains wolf or the grizzly.

The hard realities of the new grain economics may have forestalled for now the plowing of the last few precious square miles of shortgrass prairie, but that alone will not ensure the survival of the animals which cling to life there. The experimental station at Onefour once saved the people who live here from the ravages of booster dreams and unchecked development, and as this century of settlement and consolidation closes, it is not the future of humans in this place which is at risk. Rather it is the future of every other living thing that must coexist here with them that hangs in the balance. Perhaps this is the time to put Onefour's mothballed facilities and its flexible minds back to work on a different set of problems.

Cultivators of the earth are the most valuable citizens.
—THOMAS JEFFERSON

BORDERLINE TOWNS

*A*t the end of March, it already feels like full spring has come to the Milk River Ridge. Temperatures during the day are those of mid-June or July, and for the first time the radio weatherman is predicting a night without frost. On the temporary ponds which fill every small depression, the first spring migrants—widgeon, pintail and common golden-eye—are beginning to gather. The pearl gray male northern harriers are back, too, stunting low over the fields, but in their talons they are as likely to be carrying nest-building sticks as mice or voles. Flocks of tundra swans feed on the larger ponds, and great mists of snow geese swirl and circle overhead, but they won't stay here long. A few bald eagles and even fewer of their larger golden cousins drift on the building thermals. The bald eagles are headed back into the high country. The goldens will stay to nest in the coulees and along the Milk River Ridge, but only where there is even less than this sparse human presence. There are lots of soaring buteos, but their white undersides and dark wrist patches mark them as rough-legged hawks overwintering here from their nesting grounds in the high Arctic. They are moving slowly north, to be replaced over the next fortnight by the first waves of Swainson's and red-tailed, the common summer residents of the southern prairies.

The surface signs of spring are strong, but the land is still a spare monochrome of stubble gold, and the few trees are still leafless skeletons. On the shoulders of the ridge, the sun may be blinding, but it is still too low in the sky, even at noon, to reach the snow in the gullies and roadside ditches. It is warm, even hot, in the sun, but in the shade the air has not warmed, and the breeze still has a bite to it.

The Milk River is already clear and dropping after the first runoff. It will rise again when the higher mountain snows begin to melt, but that will be brief and likely unspectacular. In the town of Milk River and on the surrounding highways, there is a sense of heightened activity. Trucks are everywhere, moving livestock, grain or irrigation pipe. A few are pulling white tanks of anhydrous ammonia fertilizer, delivering them to the outlying farms. There is activity everywhere but in the fields. The huge eight-wheel tractors are still in their Quonsets, and most of the fields look much like they did after the final pass of the combines the previous fall. It's too early to seed; the ground is too cold for germination, and on the north-facing slopes of the undulating fields, it's probably still frozen. More snow in the next six weeks is a certainty.

Milk River has a steady, prosperous look. A new subdivision of decidedly upscale ranch bungalows occupies the high ground at the north end, and down toward the center of town, near a short line of new townhouses, a sizable new Catholic church has already replaced the one that recently burned.

Crowned with a huge cross, it shows the traditional gothic stone-and-brick facade. But, in a concession to modern methods and contemporary economics, the masonry is a veneer over a wood frame. The main north–south street is flanked on both sides by rows of what used to be called mobile homes. With their tidy lawns and sun decks, gardens and paved driveways, they long ago gave up any pretense of mobility, looking now every bit as established as the neat, clapboard houses which line the cross streets. Like almost every other rural town its size, Milk River has its small RCMP detachment, its golf course and an old commercial hotel to house its tavern. There is a well-stocked supermarket, a bakery, a drugstore and a real estate office. Out by the highway, across from the big elevators, are the farm implement dealers, the UFA office, the gas stations and a long, low, one-story motel.

Milk River has a new hospital, and the construction of a new extended-care wing has only just been finished. What used to be the Border Counties General Hospital now goes by the bland, modern name of the Milk River & District Health Centre. Out by the grain elevators, though, where the traffic passes along Highway 4 toward Lethbridge or Great Falls, one of those portable backlit signs favored by strip-mall merchants is advertising for doctors. Milk River may have new medical facilities, but it has a hard time finding staff. The town hall is modern and the provincial tourist information building is new. Yet it wasn't the tax revenues from a prospering town which built the town hall or moved the Alberta government to provide the new hospital. It's all royalty money from oil and gas in a town which has little of either close to hand. And it's oil and gas money which has begun to dry up.

In the restaurant at the Southgate Motel, the regular morn-

ing coffee klatch is well under way by 7:30 A.M. Though the
faces change, the number at the table seems set at seven. They
come and go in the ubiquitous pickup truck, and the preference
is clearly for the fullest expression of the form: forty thousand
dollars of big V8 diesel 4x4s with extended cabs, long boxes
and dual rear wheels under flared fenders. The waitress keeps
the white thermoses of coffee and the cups of hot chocolate
coming. Some of the group are still working their land. Others
have already sold out or turned it over to a son or daughter and
retired to town, driving out to lend a hand during planting or
harvest and offering advice, sometimes appreciated but more
often accepted with patience and a tight smile. It's always hard
to let go of a lifetime's work.

The chat is relaxed and light-hearted, like conversation
among old friends anywhere, but the small talk and the social
news invariably give way to *the business*, a business, they all seem
to accept, which is on the cusp of huge changes. There has
been a new federal budget, and years of argument and speculation about the future of King Wheat have all come down to
one simple fact: the ancient Crow Rate is finally gone. There
was always hope it would survive, that the century-old policy of
export subsidies would retain its immunity from the realities of
the New World, but deep in their hearts they all knew it would
go, that it *had* to go.

The Milk River country was built on what it could export,
built on wheat and cows shipped out by train and truck for
processing somewhere else. The wheat, insulated by its Crow
Rate subsidy, went north to the railway main lines, then east
and west to saltwater ports and the international grain trade.
The cattle went to the Lethbridge auction markets on the hoof
and were knocked down to feedlots and packers which might

be anywhere but here. The end of the Crow Rate will not alter the relationship between these two near-solitudes, but it will be a catalyst, accelerating the economic and government policy changes which are already sweeping across this country and across the whole of the Prairie West.

Two simple absolutes determined the placement of western settlements like Milk River: how far a locomotive could travel between stops for water and fuel or how far a man in a wagon could travel in half a day, do his business and sleep in his own bed that night. The second was about ten miles.

Cultural geographers have done the hard arithmetic. A family of five on every quarter section yields a density of twenty people per square mile, giving any town within a ten-mile radius four thousand potential customers, easily enough to keep it prosperous. But as homestead sizes increased to a full section, that number dropped by seventy-five percent. With so few men, women and children to count on, no town could expect to attract merchants, railroad spurs or grain elevators, let alone collect the taxes to build roads and bridges, pay teachers or publish booster pamphlets.

The cold numbers say that even under ideal circumstances most of the towns which sprang up across the drylands were doomed to wither as the small homesteads were abandoned or consolidated. Even the railway spurs could not have saved them. Other places, those which managed by fiat or entrepreneurial zeal to bring their dreams into the thirties or forties, would be stripped from the maps as the tractor and the automobile replaced the horse. Tractors meant that fewer men could work more land, further reducing population densities; the car and the truck changed the distances over which the day's business could be done, and the miles between settlements increased accordingly.

So far Milk River has not begun to go the way of so many other towns along the northern tier.

The faded, wind-tattered Stars and Stripes which flies over the campground shows the fifteen stars of Thomas Jefferson's presidency. The stars mark the state of the Union at the beginning of the fifteen-year period when this part of Canada was legally an American possession. Drawing the 49th parallel across the high plains may have cost the United States its title to this place, but from the very beginning of white history until well into this century, the American presence in Alberta's Milk River country was pervasive.

The standard public school social studies saga of the opening of the Canadian West cannot be taught about this place; it simply doesn't apply. There were no voyageurs here, no brave explorers, no trainloads of hope-driven Galicians or Ruthenians, no thick Scottish or Maritime accents. Fort Benton was the first capital of this country, and the Whoop-Up Trail was its first highway. Milk River buffalo robes were traded south for American whiskey; the earliest Canadian letters went back east with American postage and Montana postmarks. When settlers finally came, they were Americans, and not fresh-off-the-boat Ellis Islanders, either. The ranchers came overwhelmingly from Texas and the Dakotas, the homesteaders from Wisconsin and Minnesota, Iowa and Kansas. And especially from Utah.

Since 1887 when the first ten Mormon families came north to escape their increasingly restricted lives around the Great Salt Lake, the townscapes south of Lethbridge have been dominated not by the onion-domed orthodox churches of central Alberta but by the thin, mock-gothic spires of the Latter-day Saints. Adherents to this most purely American of faiths were led by a son-in-law of Brigham Young himself. They were the first to take on the wholesale settlement of deep southern Alberta, lacing the country with their irrigation canals, their churches and their fundamental conservatism. Today, they represent the upper Milk River country's dominant social and political force. It's a given that the larger centers of Raymond and Magrath are "Mormon" towns, but even in the tiny hamlet of Del Bonita, the school and the post office–general store are dominated by a grand Latter-day Saints church and community center. It's not that the thing is ostentatious—Mormon buildings are quite austere in their own way—it's just so much bigger than anything else in town. There is a new church going up in Coutts, too, capping a low rise beside the highway at the north end of town. It was supposed to be in Milk River, but church leaders and town councilors clashed over the selection of the site, and Milk River remains the only town of any size for miles around without an obvious Mormon presence. The great temple at Cardston serves as the spiritual and administrative center of Latter-day Saints life on both sides of the border, and it seems this faith has become almost the only common ground left between Albertans and Montanans of the Milk River country.

It's fewer than fifteen miles from Milk River to the international border, but in this country the 49th parallel now marks a more than arbitrary line across the plains. Cross it at any of the four portals contained within the arc of the river, and despite a long, common history, the fact that these are two different nations is obvious even to the most casual observer. It's more than the immediacy of the change from metric speed limits or the appearance of "Cold Beer Ahead" billboards. Such things are just superficial manifestations of the deeper differences which pervade every aspect of contemporary life along the Milk.

At the Coutts–Sweetgrass crossing, the new two-lane pavement of Alberta's Highway 4 widens and deteriorates into Interstate 15, which runs without interruption to Los Angeles via Butte, Salt Lake City and Las Vegas. There is nowhere near sufficient traffic north of Great Falls to justify all this asphalt; there would have been even less when it was built in the fifties and sixties. Still, the interstate system had its Cold War standards, and Interstate 15 got four lanes, long cloverleafs to nowhere and, by midsummer, weeds growing two-feet high through the cracks in the paved shoulders.

Coutts, Alberta, is sustained by the border business, and most of its three or four hundred residents have some direct connection with the huge volumes of truck and rail traffic which have made this the busiest port of entry between Minneapolis and Seattle. There is no substantial business district in Coutts, only grids of small, neat houses clustered around a water tower radiating the inane grin of a happy-face paint job. There is no string of gas stations or tourist stops along Highway 4 above the crossing, and U.S. drivers clearing customs accelerate quickly on the divided highway and settle in for the hour or so it will take to get to Lethbridge. For the cars and trucks coming south, headed for Salt Lake or Phoenix, Coutts gets lost beside a welter of directional and cautionary signage, and most drivers don't make a rest stop before they have made the two-hour run to Great Falls.

At the border, warning signs, high chain link fences and sophisticated electronics protect one side of the line from the other, but it is far from impermeable. Next to a new and decidedly upscale children's playground in Coutts, the softball diamond is hard against the 49th parallel. There is nothing to prevent American children from using the swings, and catching a foul ball could easily involve an implicit act of international cooperation. Exploring Coutts one day, I found myself driving past a string of parked cars, all of which bore Montana tags. Somehow, and I never figured out just how, I had managed to drive unannounced into the United States. Thinking that try-ing to retrace my route and making a second unauthorized crossing might be a bad idea, I began the complicated process of getting legally back into Canada. Since you can't drive to U.S. customs from the Montana side, I drove out to the inter-state and up to the Canada Customs stop. A careful outline of the problem to an officer drew the recommendation that I drive back to the U.S. side and explain what had happened. The Americans, seeming more amused than annoyed, sent me straight back north where the same Canada Customs officer waved me past the waiting cars with a smile. It must have been obvious to all concerned that mine was too foolish a story to be anything but the truth.

Sweetgrass, Montana, is in the border business, too. Its slightly shabby collection of buildings hugs the west side of the interstate hard against the border. Other than the customs buildings and the line of identical, red brick government bun-galows, it's home to a few bars and motels, a convenience store—gas station and a large duty-free operation, the billboards for which appear everywhere along the highway between Leth-bridge and Butte. At the crossing, a large complex of collector lanes, parking lots and warning signs has replaced the original row of customs houses, which now stand fenced off and isolat-ed between the highway and the railway tracks.

Surrounded by the empty, rolling hills of the high plains, the place still manages something of a romantic air. Interstate 15 is an asphalt funnel concentrating northbound traffic from every major highway system on this side of the Mississippi, and the license plates on the cars and semitrailers lined up at the crossing come from every western state and province and a dozen more besides. Alternating with the "Big Sky" of Montana and Alberta's "Wild Rose Country" are New Mexico's "Land of Enchantment," Arizona's "Grand Canyon State," Idaho's "Famous Potatoes" and Utah's no-nonsense invitation to "Ski!" Most surprising at first notice are the ochre and blue plates of "The Last Frontier" attached to a steady stream of RVs and truck campers from Alaska. This is their last stop in the lower forty-eight on the road to the start of the Alcan Highway west of Edmonton. The big tractor-trailers have been pulling their cargoes through this portal since the United States Army began construction of the Alaska Highway during the early days of World War II. North of Sweetgrass, there are over two thousand miles of Canada between the truckers and vacationers and their destinations in Anchorage or Fairbanks.

Just visible above the benchland buttes, the peaks of the Lewis Range in Glacier Park define the horizon sixty miles or so west of Interstate 15. To the east, across Wilsall Flats, the volcanic stocks of the Sweetgrass Hills dominate the surrounding plains, their softer, rounded forms gently asserting their lack of common ancestry with the ragged skyline to the west. The country is given to grass and wheat, and dotted with hundreds of small pump jacks. The jacks are parked above the Sweetgrass Arch, drawing up what is left of the sour crude fifteen hundred feet down in the Madison limestones of the Kevin–Sunburst field.

In the sixty miles from the border to the town of Conrad the interstate crosses a series of aging oil fields, most of which were wildcat discoveries in the 1920s. Today, the operations are small, the pumpers stripping the last few barrels a day from the shallow fields. There is little sign of new investment; the paint on the pump jacks is peeling, and the small clusters of nearby storage tanks are rusting and dented. Many of the jacks stand idle and others lie in pieces, their working life over.

The big post-war plays in Montana oil and gas weren't in Milk River country. They were in the Williston basin near the North Dakota border or down in the southeast corner toward Ekalaka. The exploration fever which gripped America during the OPEC embargoes of the seventies made Billings, not Great Falls or Conrad, the main beneficiary of the brief boom that followed. The town of Kevin is what's left of oil prosperity on the Sweetgrass Arch.

Kevin isn't a ghost town. Yet. The latest road atlas gazetteer credits it with 185 souls. As I drive west from the interstate on Highway 215, about twenty miles below the border, the first sight of Kevin is a forest of rusting pipe that was once a modest-sized oil refinery. Facing it across 215 is a line of half a dozen small houses, all identical, built for the refinery workers and all abandoned. Around the refinery and the houses and over to the deserted well service businesses along the Burlington Northern right-of-way the ground is littered with worn-out trucks, rusted pipe and the general rubbish of a place which has fallen by the wayside. Tanker trucks are still the most common sight on the quiet roads, picking up the two or three barrels a day that each of the pumpers still produces, but they no longer carry their cargo to Kevin.

The singularity of the country makes cattle and wheat and oil and gas the common denominators along both sides of the 49th parallel, but the old connections have been broken. Life today on each side of the line seems to go on largely without regard to the other's existence. KSEN, the radio station which serves the Shelby–Cut Bank area, and the local stations from Lethbridge rarely make mention of anything on the other side of the border. The same holds true to the east with Medicine Hat's CHAT and Havre's KOJM. Though it's usually easy enough to follow the weather reports for a hundred miles to the north or south of wherever you are, it takes an exception to the rule, a man-bites-dog story, to make the media on one side of the line pay much attention to the other. Scanning the daily papers confirms the impression that the only cross-border stories likely to make the news are those which came in on the Associated or Canadian Press wires.

About the only time in recent history Americans and Canadians in Milk River country paid attention to each other was in the early 1990s. With a high Canadian dollar, the free trade pact and a new goods and services tax, cross-border shopping became an instant institution almost everywhere there was an American town within reasonable reach of Canada. On the high plains, cities like Great Falls saw the flow of northern shoppers as a boon to their declining economies. Great Falls is only a three-hour drive from the nearly sixty thousand residents of Lethbridge and an effortless weekend trip for nearly seven hundred and fifty thousand Calgarians.

At the peak of the cross-border mania, slick commercials began appearing on television stations across southern Alberta; newspapers and mailbox flyers touted the cheaper prices for such things as major appliances, stereos and televisions. Great Falls merchants, motel and bar owners offered improved services, special discounts and new malls, tying the shopping to a full weekend of entertainment at such places as the Charlie Russell Museum. The Calgary, Lethbridge and Medicine Hat media began to make regular pilgrimages to report on the progress of the seduction.

Still, the brief boom did not change Great Fall much. It has been said that Great Falls is a city in a state which does not like cities, and today it has the look of a place which no longer counts as much as it used to. In the downtown core, there are a few undistinguished high-rise glass cubes, but they reflect the two- and three-story surroundings of a place which peaked in the 1950s. The wonderfully nostalgic neon signs on the bars and stores have been preserved only by quiet times. Beside Park Drive, along the south bank of the Missouri, the grand old station of the Mil- waukee Railroad with its clock tower, dark brown brickwork and red tile roof has been boarded up for a long time, a comment both on the demise of the great railways and on the lack of capi- tal. In larger cities, the station would already have been subjected to the mandatory conversion into upscale boutiques and coffee shops. All but boarded up, too, is the source of Great Falls' last sustained economic stability. Malmstrom Air Force Base—with its wonderful, apocalypse-evoking name and its Strategic Air Command B—52s—was an early victim of the thawing Cold War.

Great Falls had always been there in the minds of southern Albertans. A steady five hours south of Calgary, it is the logical first stop for fuel and lunch on the long run down Interstate 15 to Salt Lake City, Phoenix or Los Angeles, and Alberta license plates were always a common sight on the forty-block strip of gas stations, motels and fast-food franchises. When Western Airlines was the main carrier for Calgarians flying into the states, Great Falls was an automatic stop on flights to and from its Salt Lake City hub. Years ago, when Alberta's blue-stockings still held sway, Great Falls was a big city, a place where liquor and Sunday shopping were easy to get.

Looking north of the border to revitalize its sputtering economy was something which made sense to the Great Falls Chamber of Commerce, for it is Alberta which has boomed almost steadily in the years since Great Falls peaked. Lethbridge now outstrips it both in population and vitality, and Calgary, in the past quarter-century, has grown to be the largest city anywhere on the northern plains by several hundreds of thousands. Indeed, the city of Calgary now boasts a population almost equal to the entire state of Montana.

Montana tourism authorities continue their smooth, generic tourism campaign to draw Albertans south, but recently the bloom has come off the cross-border rose. As the Canadian dollar slumped and the Alberta boom eroded into recession, it was no longer worth the cost—the gas, the motel, the ten-hour round trip—to buy a new refrigerator in Great Falls. Even if one could afford a refrigerator at all.

As the TV advertisements and other Great Falls promotions withered away, Montana returned to its accustomed place on the back burner of Alberta's consciousness, to be roused again only in early 1994. Interest this time was fired not by the competition for upscale consumer dollars but by the more traditional currency of the Milk River country: wheat and cows. Suddenly, the town of Shelby and the border crossing at Sweetgrass became the surprise lead story on newscasts across Canada and the United States.

Overnight, wheat—mostly hard southern Alberta durum bound for the newly fashionable pasta makers south of the line—replaced West Coast softwood and cedar shingles as the *cause celebre* in a series of free trade battles over Canadian commodities. Shelby was back in the spotlight for the first time since Jack Dempsey's heavyweight title-fight debacle of 1923.

Shelby, a town of perhaps twenty-five hundred, lies along the Hi-Line where it crosses Interstate 15 about thirty miles south of Sweetgrass. It's here that the old Great Northern main line between Chicago and Seattle intersects the north–south spur running down to Great Falls and here that the line of grain elevators overflows with Canadian durum.

It took a fifty-two-year-old Shelby farmer to blow the smoldering dispute into flame when, in January 1994, he pulled his grain truck across the entrance to the elevators, effectively barricading them against any more Canadian wheat. Hank Zell's problem was simple: with the elevators filled with Canadian wheat, there was nowhere for his own grain to go and no way to get paid for it. Though it was still early in the year, Zell was looking ahead to harvesttime and the prospect of his already overflowing storage bins.

Zell's concerns may have been pragmatic and personal at the outset, but the larger issues of free trade and the high demand for Canadian durum in the United States quickly escalated the fight. Seeing a helpful test case in the making, a high-level trade panel made it all the way from Washington D.C. to hear the local farmers out, and Zell himself, by midsummer an emerging media personality, ended up in his nation's capital for a meeting with the Secretary of Agriculture. The press was having a field day, and for the first time in quite a while, everyone had something to say about the goings-on across the line.

As the debate dragged on toward the harvest, with government officials in Ottawa and Washington making all sorts of get-tough promises to their constituents, nagging fears about the free trade deal among farmers and ranchers, both north and south, began to bubble to the surface again. To Montanans unable to get their wheat into the elevators, Canadian cereals, with their heavy subsidies, were going to put them out of business. To the Canadians, America's farmers, flush with their own subsidy programs and unable to meet the growing demand for top-quality durum, were trying to keep them out of the market in order to push prices up. It was easy to find farmers and ranchers north of the border who would tell you that anything the United States had been so eager to sign wasn't going to be good for anyone but the Americans. If there was any agreement at all to be found along the old Medicine Line in the summer of 1994, it was that the free trade deal was turning out to be no deal at all.

Like it or not, Hank Zell and his ongoing crusade have brought some of the long-dormant border jealousies back into play and reminded the two solitudes of Milk River country of the old connections between them. Tight economies and tough times on both sides of the border mean that this will be just another battle in the long series which began with the fur trappers, whiskey traders and cattle barons more than a century ago.

Everyone in Alberta likes to say the easy times are over, and they have taken up preaching economy and miserly austerity with the same missionary zeal they once brought to spending. This will soon matter to a town like Milk River, which has a certain artificiality about it, a sense that it has been sheltered from the hard realities of life in this dry land. The Shelbys and Kevins and Havres have risen and fallen on the changing fortunes of a bushel of wheat or a barrel of oil and lived with Montana's laissez-faire philosophy of low taxes and equally low services. By contrast, the small towns of Alberta have almost been guaranteed a living. North of the line, backstopped by its multibillion-dollar Heritage Fund, Alberta pursued a philosophy of low taxes and high services, settling on the principle that every citizen, no matter how isolated, should benefit equally from its boundless oil and gas revenues. In the good times, there were new hospitals to be had almost for the asking. There were paved roads and huge dams. There were parks, museums and interpretive centers for every small place which wanted them (and almost all of them did). And when the good times went bad, there were endless initiatives for tourism and public works, huge loan guarantees for any harebrained scheme which looked like it might create jobs. When falling oil prices froze the Heritage Fund, Albertans were easily weaned onto government borrowing to cover their subsidies and blue-sky visions. And, when the debt became an embarrassment even to the most shameless of political spenders, the old addiction to easy money shifted to video lotteries and casino gambling. But it can't do on.

For the first time since the Great Depression, Milk River will be facing the world without the protection of a beneficent provincial government. It will have to deal with an aging population, which is seeing its income supports and medical exemptions steadily eroded. It will have to come up with the money to maintain the expensive public works—the water and waste treatment plants—which government capital so generously provided. It will have to find ways to keep at least some of its young people at home and provide for their education. It will have to keep its businesses alive against the rivalry of other towns which are facing the same new need to compete or die.

For now, Milk River is a town that seems at ease with itself. It has lived for years with its nine hundred souls. Never subjected to the wild extremes of oil and gas boomers or the mad rush of the homesteaders, it has the feel of a place that will always be here. Milk River got its railway and its elevators. It got a main highway and steady border traffic. It retained a surrounding market area which mixed cattleman and farmer. And it had the river. When the droughts came, it could count on the water most of the time. Far enough away from other towns to remain a convenient center for shopping and schooling and socializing, but too close to Lethbridge to grow to city status, Milk River settled comfortably into itself.

People still know each other here, and it would be hard for any resident to walk from the drugstore to the bank without greeting almost everyone along the way. The smiles of recognition from the waitresses and the counter clerks are still genuine, and everywhere there is the relaxed sense of regularity that comes from years of quiet rituals. This is a town of old friends, but of old friends growing older together. Like the rest of Canada, more than a third of Milk River's farmers are already over fifty years old, and that number will continue to climb year by year. It's significant that the new wing on the hospital is for extended care, not day care. It's important that the new Catholic church is set at ground level with no grand stairway up to the front doors. At the drugstore, a seniors' discount must amount almost to a universal benefit.

The same accidents of geography and history which first gave life to Milk River and let it survive through other tough times say it will be here for a long while yet. The border business means it will keep its railway and its elevators. The highway and the provincial park will still bring the tourists to its shops and gas stations, and the big cities remain too far away for the daily necessities.

But other small towns across the Milk River country will continue to shrink back into oblivion. They are finally losing the branch lines and elevators which let them hang on for decades after their boomer dreams had died, and everyone still too young for a pension will have to go with them. Many will be lost to declining reserves of oil. Others will shrink in the new realities of agriculture. Along the Montana Hi-Line and Alberta 61, towns like Rudyard and Kremlin, Orion, Etzikom and Manyberries will begin to disappear from the maps entirely, joining the long list of brief places soon to be lost even to memory.

Hear me my chiefs; I am tired. My heart is sick and sad.
—CHIEF JOSEPH

KOPET!

laine County, Montana, is over four thousand square miles of dryland wheat and shortgrass pasture between the 49th parallel and the Missouri River. The sixty-seven hundred souls of Blaine County inhabit a place four times as big as the state of Rhode Island and twice the size of Canada's Prince Edward Island. They are spread so thinly that even today the terms of the landmark 1890 U.S. Census would define the country as unsettled. The Hi-Line cuts across the country, closely paralleling the Milk River as they run their courses east from Havre toward Malta and Glasgow and their meeting with the Missouri below the Fort Peck dam. Below the Hi-Line, roads are few and, with the exception of Montana 66 through the Fort Belknap Reservation, almost all gravel. So empty is the southern part of this place that the sole Missouri River crossing is by the summertime-only McClelland ferry.

Fifteen hundred people, nearly a quarter of Blaine's population, live in the county seat of Chinook. A quiet farm town in its own right, it is also almost a suburb of Havre some twenty miles away to the west. South of Chinook, Montana 240 runs toward the low, slumped silhouettes of the Bears Paw Mountains, one of America's great lost places.

In the late September of 1877, a ragged and exhausted train of perhaps six hundred men, women and children crossed the Missouri River and came into this lonely country. Skirting the eastern base of the Bears Paws, they dropped down into the sheltering valley of Snake Creek. It was a biting cold day, damp and windy with the threat of snow, and here, having managed to kill a few of the last buffalo, the group subdivided into its bands and families to eat and rest.

In the previous one hundred days, with fewer than two hundred warriors, they had traveled nearly two thousand miles across mountains and rivers from their ancient home on the Idaho–Oregon border, outfighting or outrunning at every turn the best the United States Cavalry could throw at them. With what remained of the two hundred warriors to protect the women and children, the elderly and a herd of perhaps a thousand horses, they crossed into the Milk River country on their desperate flight to Canada. Their camp on Snake Creek was only two days and forty miles from the sanctuary of the Medicine Line. The pursuing soldiers, they believed, were more than that behind them.

On the cold, gray afternoon of October 5, *Hin-mah-too-yah-lat-kekht*, Thunder Rolling in the Mountains, a man the whites knew as Chief Joseph, handed his rifle to Colonel Nelson Miles and finished the epic flight of the Nez Perce. How fast it had all come and gone! Joseph's father, the great Chief Tuekakas, was already out of his teens in the year when Lewis and Clark became the first white faces the Nez Perce had ever seen, and yet he died only six years before his son began the final, futile run to freedom. Perhaps a few of the elders who crouched freezing in the shadows of the Bears Paws had actually seen the captains themselves as they came ragged and starving over the Great Divide in 1805.

Like so many of the benchmarks of western history, the flight of the Nez Perce has been boiler-plated with mythology. This time, though, the stereotypes have always run counter to the Little Bighorn or Wounded Knee. Never contaminated by pulp fiction images of bloodthirsty savage or genocidal soldier, the saga which ended in the Bears Paw Mountains has come down to us as one of enormous and noble sadness.

There is, in the demise of the Nez Perce, the usual cast of villains, from desperate homesteaders and wild-eyed prospectors to missionary zealots, Indian agents and Washington bureaucrats, but they have rarely found apologists. From the start, the *Nimipu*, as they called themselves, had been the paradigm of what the newcomers found admirable in the western Indian.

Though ravaged by early outbreaks of smallpox and cowed by the trade muskets of the Blackfeet, they nevertheless welcomed Lewis and Clark, the first whites they had ever encountered, and probably saved the Corps from death in the impossible mountains which were their home. The captains visited again on their return from the Pacific and spent perhaps five weeks with the Nez Perce, compiling vocabularies and studying tribal customs, bedding the young women and transcribing mental maps of the intermountain plateaus. The journals of their visits are filled with warmth and genuine admiration.

So it was through the nineteenth century, too, with the fur traders and missionaries, surveyors and treaty makers who judged the Nez Perce to be superbly adaptable, brilliant horsemen, ferocious but not savage warriors, generous of spirit and on and on. So it was until someone actually coveted their lands. Then, as it was everywhere else, all was forgotten.

Some of the *Nimipu* went quietly onto their small Idaho reservations, accepting the fate the whites had determined for them. Others like Joseph and White Bird and Looking Glass continued as best they could to live as they always had. Forced finally to choose between life on the reservation or death anywhere else, they elected an option of their own making: a run toward whatever freedom they hoped might still remain on the northern plains. It wasn't a guerrilla raid or some suicidal rush toward a final glory. It wasn't just the young men who ran. When the Nez Perce came over the divide, they came with everything they had—with women and children and the elderly, with their horses and lodges and their deep memories of the old ways.

Whatever they were running from, there was nothing to run to. They should have known—they must have known— that the plains were gone, that there remained only fragments of the real life. Canada was not then in their plans. There seemed some faint, dreamy hope that their old allies, the Crows, would take them in for those last few years. But the Crows had already gone under and expressed no interest in anything Nez Perce but their horses, something the whites had promised them as tribute if they helped bring the renegades to heel.

Knowing of Sitting Bull's Sioux and their retreat north across the Medicine Line to Canada, the Nez Perce caravan turned east and north toward the Missouri, the Bears Paws and Snake Creek. The image of the Nez Perce moving east, carrying all they owned into unknown territory, turns the great settlement saga on its head: the Indian, seeking his freedom, retraces the path of the white settler who had come west in search of the same thing. Nothing drives home the absolute futility of it all quite as perfectly as this: early in their trek across the newly created Yellowstone National Park, the Nez Perce captured and briefly held two parties of eastern tourists.

The details of the final stand are well known from contemporary accounts, and all seem more or less consistent. The main body of the cavalry, under General O.O. Howard, was indeed more than two days behind the Nez Perce. What Joseph and the others could not know was that Colonel Nelson A. Miles had been summoned up from Fort Keough on the Yellowstone with orders to intercept the band before it reached the border.

On the freezing morning of September 30, while the Nez Perce camp was barely awake, two prongs of Miles' cavalry poured into Snake Creek at full charge. One group went straight at the camp, the other veered off to seize the horses. The irregular topography blunted the force of both charges, and the Nez Perce, as they had everywhere along the route of their flight, took only a few moments to organize their resistance and return a withering fire. In the chaos of the moment, over two hundred men, women and children swept out of the coulees and raced north for the border. Those who remained dug themselves in along the creek and eventually forced the cavalry back onto the high ground. Miles, with a fifth of his troop killed or wounded, was unprepared to mount another assault before the arrival of the main body under Howard. He surrounded the camp and settled in to wait.

Most of those who escaped the cavalry's first charge eventually crossed into Canada to live with Sitting Bull and his expatriate Sioux, but not before seven of their number were killed on the Milk River by Assiniboine anxious to demonstrate that they wanted no part of the trouble. The faint hope that Sitting Bull would bring his warriors down to break the siege was just a fantasy. By then, the old veteran knew a futile cause when he saw one.

In the final analysis, the tactical details aren't important. What mattered was that Miles now stood between the Nez Perce and the border and that they could go no farther. At this moment, Thunder Rolling in the Mountains stepped out and made his place in history. In an instant, the historical figure of Chief Joseph and the single overarching image of the Nez Perce as a nation came into being and were fixed in a nation's consciousness.

Joseph was not a warrior. It is unlikely that he had fired a shot in anger until the morning of Miles' charge. The Nez Perce had never had a single leader, their custom being to operate by the consensus of their many chiefs. Joseph's responsibility was for the camp, for ensuring the safety of the women and children, for the day-to-day management of the horses and food supplies. He was in charge of the life of the community, and it was for the life of the community that he acted. White Bird had gone on to Canada; Looking Glass and a number of the principal warriors were dead. The children were freezing and food was almost gone. They could not run without leaving the sick and the wounded, and they could not stand another charge.

Responding to Miles' promise (honestly made) that he could take what was left of his people back to their homes across the divide, Joseph rode out of the valley and dismounted before the cavalry commanders. Speaking so softly that even those nearby could not hear him, he is said to have uttered the single most famous sentence in the whole history of the Indian West: "From where the sun now stands, I will fight no more forever."

Today, after more than a century of almost complete neglect, after living in the shadow of Custer and the Little Bighorn, the Bear's Paw Battleground is being elevated to its proper place in the history of the American West.

The new pavement of Montana 240 goes nowhere else, ending just south of the site against the flank of the Bears Paws at a gravel road between the tiny communities of Lloyd and Cleveland. Until the National Park Service took over management of the battlefield from the state, the signs on Route 2 pointing the way south from Chinook were small, faded and easy to miss. Even the site itself was almost unmarked, accessible from a small parking circle beside the road near a couple of toilets and picnic tables. By June 1993, the federal government had added a full-time ranger, who drove down from town every day to watch over the place and greet the few people who managed to find it. In October of that year, on the anniversary of Joseph's surrender, the Bears Paw Battlefield officially took its place as a part of the Nez Perce National Historic Park, a chain of sites which stretches across four states and marks the route of their final flight.

The battlefield site takes in the grassy hills and coulees of Snake Creek as it meanders its way north toward the Milk. Though there is a ranch house within sight and the battlefield is circumscribed by a barbed-wire fence, it still conveys the clear sense that this is the way it must have looked in the autumn of 1877. In the twenties, a Chinook businessman's love for history had the site excluded from the Homestead Act and saved from cattle grazing and the plow. At about the same time, a forward-thinking historian contacted Nez Perce survivors and drove them back along the route of their march, carefully recording their memories. At the Bears Paw, they hammered small stakes, like survey markers, into the grass to note the places where the families camped, where Looking Glass and Joseph's brother fell.

But for these interventions and the personal passions of a few local residents, the battlefield's remoteness was all that saved it. The Nez Perce were here for only a moment, uninvited and unwanted fugitives in a country of Blackfeet and Assiniboine, beaten warriors in a state which already boasted the grand, bloody glory of the Little Bighorn.

What will happen to the site now that it has become a national historic park is open to conjecture. Certainly, the State of Montana would have had no plans that approach what the federal government seems to have in mind. Up here on the Hi-Line, there seems an almost complete indifference to history, and it will be instructive to see how the people of Havre and Chinook will react to the new, bright light which is beginning to shine on this part of their past. It will be interesting to see what will happen to the simple eloquence that is the Bears Paw Battlefield.

One thing is certain: it must not be forced to become another Little Bighorn. That myth-riddled place has always held a huge attraction, and tens of thousands of tourists visit its heavily interpreted sites on their way between Mount Rushmore and Yellowstone Park. At the intersection of the northern plains' two main interstate highways, it is fully tourist accessible. A part of the Crow Reservation and adjoining that of the northern Cheyenne, it has served as an obvious focal point in the reemergence of native power, political and cultural. It is also a place of trinkets and T-shirt shops, a place where the pathways which crisscrossed the site have been closed and visitors' experience reduced to a series of asphalt roads and detached, set-piece vistas viewed through a car window.

The Bears Paw Battlefield site and the characters who acted out the final scenes of the Indian West are far too complex to support the simple, sentimental morality plays best suited to modern interpretation. Nothing happened here as it should have; none of the players fit the stereotypes, old or new. There was no Masada, no suicidal last stand. There was no massacre by the men of the 2nd and 7th Cavalry (a small miracle considering that so many of their comrades had fallen with Custer only a year before). There was the usual litany of broken promises, but they were broken by others, thousands of miles away. What began here with gunfire and the screams of the dying ended with a quiet dignity. What's left is a silence that drowns out the circus music of the Little Bighorn.

Perhaps for once it will occur to the powers that be, both white and native, that the people who take the time to come to this quiet, lonely place do not need or want to be told what they should think or feel. That they do not need grand interpretive centers, souvenir shops, manicured lawns or organized tours.

Whether Joseph ever spoke his most perfect sentence or any of the others in that brief, brilliant speech is a subject for ongoing debate among historians, but it really doesn't matter. It was here on the southern border of the Milk River country, along Snake Creek, hundreds of miles from his home, that Joseph pronounced an end to the magnificent buffalo cultures of the Great Plains. It was here that he handed back the guns and the horses that had made them all possible. There is a word in the Nez Perce tongue, a word that Joseph might well have used at that huge moment. *"Kopet!"* he might have said. "That is all."

To make a start in particulars and make them general.
—WILLIAM CARLOS WILLIAMS

FRAGMENTS OF THE INFINITE

The topographic map says 49° north latitude is about seven hundred yards directly south of the gravel road which runs west from Aden to Coutts, but I can see no obvious, unbroken fence line to mark it. Though the rounded crests of the Sweetgrass Hills are well within Montana, the West Butte makes its presence felt here above the line as the road is forced to climb gently but steadily across its northern flank. From the top of the rise, at over thirty-seven hundred feet, the full compass of Alberta's Milk River country is visible in one stunning sweep.

On this clear day, I can see to the northeast the low, flat-topped shimmer of the Cypress Hills. Almost as far away to the west, the Milk River Ridge is a barely perceptible swell on the horizon. Between them are 120 miles of pure space, stretching beyond the Milk and across the invisible divide to disappear, at the eye's limit, in the haze which blurs the place where the sky begins.

Across this enormous panorama, there seems not a single square foot which has not been touched—and changed forever—by the hand of man. From the shoulder of West Butte, the clichéd image of the patchwork quilt is obvious and unavoidable. Irregular, straight-sided shapes and colors that change with the season, stitched together with fence posts and wire, this is Wallace Stegner's country of geometry, a country made by twentieth-century man.

"Oceans" was the common metaphor for early travelers across the high plains—endless seas with grass for waves. Almost everywhere along the Milk River it is still possible to watch the wind whip swirling patterns away to the horizon. But turn the head slightly to either side or walk to the top of any low rise and the illusion collapses instantly, punctured by the spikes of utility poles, by fence lines, by the vapor trail of a transcontinental airliner or the column of dust roiling behind a pickup on a distant road. The oceans of shortgrass are all but gone now, and across the country the wind blows waves into dark green rectangles of spring wheat and barley, oats and alfalfa.

And yet some fragments of the infinite endure. Out on the great grazing reserves—on Twin River, Sage Creek and Pinhorn—the echoes of what the high plains once were still resonate clearly across the hills and coulees. Here, and only here, on 186,000 acres of native grass, it seems possible to turn your back to the road and walk away into history. There are still herds of pronghorn here, and coyote and grouse. There are deer and burrowing owls, even swift foxes. Everything appears to be the way it used to be.

For all the appearance of wilderness, though, these public lands are not wild places. The grazing reserves are not parks, and they do not exist to remind us of the buffalo or the Blackfeet. Like center-post irrigators and alternating strips of wheat and fallow, the grazing reserves are a carefully managed response to the need to coax a living from this dry country. And more than anything else, they are a compromise between the old agrarian dreams and the reality of what the land will allow. They are also the last hope for saving the shortgrass prairie.

East from Aden, east from 880, past the few scattered ranch houses, past Black Butte and the Canadian Montana gas plant, the good gravel road gives way to smooth ruts of packed dirt. Perhaps fifteen miles in, the track makes a hard right turn and drops like a plumb line toward the border and a single lonely homeplace that misses being American by only a couple of hundred yards. Straight on from the turn, the roadside fences and ditches disappear, the track narrows to dry-weather passable and ends at the weathered sign announcing the western boundary of the Pinhorn Grazing Reserve. Away to the southwest, the Sweetgrass Hills still dominate the horizon, and far ahead the Cypress Hills seem closer than they should be. The bracketing hills are the only reference points on the gently rolling landscape of pure shortgrass, the only physical evidence that this place does not go on forever.

The tidy fences which mark the boundaries of the huge grazing pastures come and go beside the track as it winds north then east into the heart of the lower Pinhorn. This land has never suffered the indignity of the plow, never been turned upside down and forced into wheat. The Spencer Brothers ran cows down here before the turn of the century, and when the province moved to create the reserve in 1961, the range was home to livestock wearing the venerable brand of the old Bar–N–Bar, first seen up around Manyberries in the early days of ranching in the Milk River country. But for the natural gas, this has always been pure cattle country. Even the name of the place—Pinhorn—seems perfectly evocative, some local nickname for the antelope that thrive here. But like appearances, names can be deceptive. Pinhorn is not named for the antelope but for a veterinarian, one Doc Pinhorn, who ran the quarantine station in this country when the Mounted Police first began to enforce the rules against Montana cattle grazing free on the Canadian rangelands.

The maps show that just beneath the surface this range is laced with the pipelines of the Canadian Montana Gas Company, a wholly owned possession of Montana Power. While the flanks of the Sweetgrass Hills are dotted with the small, aging oil pump jacks that characterize the Montana border country, they are a rare sight in this corner of Alberta. It's almost as if the Medicine Line had drawn a geological as well as a political reality: oil below the border, gas above it. The geometric grid of pipelines feeds the processing plant at Black Butte and the main camp below Pakowki Lake at Pendant d'Oreille. In a nod to the history of this place, nearly all of the Milk River's gas is piped south across the line to supplement Montana's chronically inadequate domestic production.

The gas company has been here since 1950 when the demands of the Korean War on the Anaconda Company's huge smelters proved more than Montana Power could meet. Albertans had known about the five pools of gas near Pakowki Lake, but they were too small to warrant bringing the pipelines south, and permits were issued to allow their export in the cause of the war effort. Milk River gas began to move across the line in 1952, and after the war the permits were extended to allow for Canadian Montana's continued presence.

Through the fifties, the pipelines spread out from Pendant

d'Oreille, bringing in gas from Manyberries and Comrey and Foremost, pumping it south across the border near Aden and into the Montana grid. Black Butte, with its compressors and dehydrators, was built in 1960, a new compressor station for Aden was added a year later and the main camp at Pendant d'Oreille was steadily expanded and improved. Unlike the oil pumpers with their storage tanks and faint, sulfurous smells, the gas moves beneath the grass, invisible save for the scattered markers where the lines cross under the hardpan road, preserving for the eye at least the sense of wildness in this place.

From the faded sign, the hardpan track undulates across the low, rounded hills, skirting the ragged tears of the narrow coulees and the seasonal ponds. So unrelentingly regular and even is the geography of this place that almost nothing bears a name. Exposed along the coulee banks beneath the thin veneer of grass, the newest of a thousand feet and more of Cretaceous sediments are stacked in their complex of parallel lines like giant stone walls. The gravels and gray muds have weathered to a muted palette of creamy ochres shot through with pale iron reds and soft oranges.

Except in springtime when the new grass is an implausible golf-course green and the wet rocks reflect a full rainbow of rich, earthy tones, this country is a quiet, shimmering monochrome. Unbroken by the rich, bold green of trees or the aggressive black of mountain rock, the colors of this place are painted by a constant, drying wind and an unrelenting sun that work against contrast at every turn. Even the huge blue sky bleaches to near-white as the sun moves toward noon. Against the pale backdrop of sandstones and drying grasses, the sagebrush and the prickly pear cactus add a subtle counterpoint of soft silver-blues and greens. Even the late spring flowers are more subtle in color than the rich, exotic riot which is the mark of their mountain relatives.

Nearly every living thing that makes a home on the short-grass prairie works to blend into this austere canvas. Soft and mottled, the colors of the shortgrass camouflage prey against predator, as they are just as surely the ally of those same preda-tors. Pale and reflective, the colors are protection from the burning sun. The prairie falcons and the Krider's red-tailed, the harriers and the great ferruginous hawks, the pale sparrows and longspurs, the coyotes and swift foxes, the sage grouse, the bur-rowing owls and the pocket gophers show a hundred combina-tions of sandy brown and gray on white. Shining white below and light butterscotch above, the pronghorn antelope can be all but invisible against a drygrass slope, revealing its presence only when silhouetted against the sky from the crest of a ridge or the rim of a cutbank.

The birds and animals of the open plains are quiet, too, in their voices, a camouflage of sound that mimics the rustling of the wind through the grass. Out on the Pinhorn, the wind is a white noise, so steady and understated that the mind mistakes it for dead silence. As the summer deepens, the bright mating songs of the shortgrass sparrows fade to variations on a theme of dry chips and buzzing whirrs more reminiscent of insects than birds. Against the constant background hiss, the raspy screech of a soaring hawk comes in softly from miles away, its source no more than a distant speck against the huge sky. But for the whistle of the ground squirrel, the yip of the coyote or the occasional soft, sharp bark of the pronghorn, but for the elegant, crystal clear cadence of the western meadowlark, the boldest sound of the shortgrass country might be no more than the dull roar of the blood through your own veins.

But the brief, familiar bawl of a cow to her calf is another reminder that this is no longer a truly wild place. The government calls the Pinhorn natural grassland, and so in its way it is. At least it's as natural as any grassland can be after nearly a hundred years of agricultural occupation. The land may never have been plowed, and to the eye it looks right, but it is certain that any ground-level, square-by-square analysis of what is growing here would reveal how much things have changed since the buffalo grazed this endless ocean. The wind has blown the seeds of change onto the Pinhorn and built a hybrid grassland, a crossbred mix of species ancient and introduced. Mixed among the native grasses are crested wheatgrass, Russian thistle and yellow clover. The Pinhorn will never again be exactly what it was for the thousands of years before the turn of this century.

And there is too much water here, more than Nature intended. The coulee bottoms ought to be bone-dry, not rich with dark water, ringed by reeds and speckled with flotillas of ducks. The managers of the Pinhorn have worked to gather and hold water everywhere there was a chance, building small dams and dugouts to ensure that their cattle can always get to water. Everywhere that the ponds show the promise of surviving beyond the brief plenty of spring, the migrating ducks and shoreline waders have been drawn unerringly to them.

Like the shiny black surface of the ponds, the bold colors and raucous calls of the waterfowl seem out of place against the sere palette of the surrounding hills. Shaded behind a bright new sign proclaiming that some tiny lake has been made possible through the cooperative efforts of the range managers and Ducks Unlimited, the beginning birder can add the prairie ducks to his new life-list one after another. Pintails and canvasbacks, ring-bills and redheads, shovelers, grebes and coots all bob and dance across the precious water. Marbled godwits and spindly, elegant avocets pace the shallows, probing the muddy bottom with long needle bills. How the divers and dabblers and shoreline waders find these tiny sanctuaries is a wonder, but at the height of the spring migration not one will escape their attention. Some of the birds, closing on the end of their annual travels, are only resting for a short time. Others will stay the summer to nest in the green shelter of the cattails and long grasses which mark the wet margins of the ponds.

The track ends in a tight circle before a small wooden cabin and a collection of corrals. South of the river, this is the place to where the cows and their calves are trucked in the spring and turned loose onto the huge pastures. In the fall, somewhere about mid-October, they are rounded up and brought back to the waiting trucks, headed back to their home-places for a winter of feeding on the grass and grain which has grown in the bottomlands in their absence.

The corrals and the cabin are the only signs of human activity for as far as the eye can see. In earlier times, the cabin might have meant life itself for a Spencer Ranch cowboy caught out here in a February blizzard. Today, it is where the pickup truck gives way once again to the horse, where the big diesel transporters meet the old open range.

The compound ought to bring a human scale to this place. It should give me some precise reference point from which to take the measure of the horizon in terms I can grasp, but it has exactly the opposite effect. Viewed from just a hundred yards or so away, the land has already begun to swallow it up, dwarfing it to something of no more consequence than a rock or a sage bush. Barely enough to bend the wind, one low-slung assemblage of wood and wire does not announce that this country is here for the taking. Rather it speaks quietly to the fact that life on the shortgrass is a great compromise forged solely on terms of Nature's making.

A few miles from the cabin, the canyon of the Milk River cuts its ragged, spectacular way across the full breadth of the Pinhorn. From the lip of the north rim, near the old ranch compound which serves as reserve headquarters, the canyon reduces its tiny stream to insignificance. Nearly five hundred feet below the rim, the Milk River snakes back and forth across the bottom of the gorge, striving to continue the steady progress down toward China begun twelve thousand years ago by the vast glacial flood which tore this gash into the bottomless sediments. Today, the river barely makes an impression on the canyon floor. Even with the addition of Montana water, the river's flow cannot sweep away the sand and gravels which wash down from the decaying walls of the gulches and coulees. Slowly, infinitely slowly, the great canyon of the Milk River is growing wider and shallower.

Viewed from the canyon rim, the Milk presents a series of textbook illustrations on the dynamics of the plains river. Water needs to run straight downhill, along some non-negotiable line of least resistance, and it will grind ceaselessly toward that end. Blocked by some obstruction, some rock or harder sediment, it will bend around and settle temporarily for another route, but it never stops wanting to go that first way. The complex meanders of the Milk are the marks of a work perpetually in progress.

The constantly evolving shape of the river is evident everywhere. On its present course along the broad canyon bottom, the riverbanks are rough and sheer but no more than a foot or two deep, a microcosm of the great canyon through which it runs. One after another, abandoned oxbows show as crescent-shaped depressions, like pale, sandy bows tied to the ribbon of green water. Along these shallow fringes, where the river used to flow, scrub willows and bunches of grass still cling tenaciously to life, drawing up what little moisture might still be here and waiting for the short, sharp rises that follow the thunderstorms or the spring runoff. When the river comes up that way, quickly and violently, it will overrun its course and briefly fill the oxbows again. It will be just enough to keep the willows through another season.

As with the impounds and ponds which dot the uplands, there is more water in the canyon than there ought to be. Tiny and inconsequential as it may seem from five hundred feet up on the rim, the Milk is a giant compared to what it would be without the Spider Coulee siphons. The addition of St. Mary water keeps the river steadily higher than it would naturally be, accelerating the pace of the river's work, giving a constancy that it would not normally enjoy. It cuts its banks faster and deeper, keeps the ground a little wetter and grows its bankside shrubs a little higher. It is the St. Mary water that seeps into the loose gravels and dried muds and creates the patches of quicksand that lurk along the river's edge, waiting to trap the occasional deer or cow that wanders down to drink. Like the grass ranges of the Pinhorn, the river bottom is not as wild and natural as the eye might first believe.

In its glossy promotional literature, the Alberta government paints a welcoming picture of places like the Pinhorn, making much of the fact that these are public lands owned by all of its citizens and open for them to use. There are caveats— gentle warnings that the grazing of cattle is the principal purpose of the reserves and suggestions that other public uses are best pursued in the winter months when the cows are back on their homeplaces. Still, the Pinhorn and Sage Creek draw their autumn share of hunters. This is prime country for deer and antelope and upland birds.

Hunters have always known about these places and they are a regular destination for university field trips, biological studies and boy scout camp-outs. But to people not involved in the ranching business, to city-dwelling Albertans from somewhere other than Lethbridge or Medicine Hat, the Pinhorn and Sage Creek and Twin River ranges simply do not exist. They are unmarked on any standard road map. Even the most detailed topographics make no mention of them. Where they are bounded or crossed by major roadways, there are few signs to indicate their presence and none encouraging the traveler to stop. There are no campsites, no amenities and no marked trails. Still, in slowly growing numbers, urban Albertans are finding the Pinhorn and discovering the great canyon of the Milk River.

Canoeing guides usually relegate the Milk River to the back of the book, almost an afterthought to the mountain glories of the Bow and the Athabasca or family-friendly, civilized badlands adventures along the Red Deer. The guides give the Milk a mixed billing, uncertain as to whether its lack of whitewater makes it a more or less desirable undertaking. They are serious in their warnings about the snags, sandbars and quicksand and careful in locating precisely the barbed-wire ranch fences strung across the river at the unintentionally perfect height to garrote a kneeling paddler.

The books take the measuring of the river seriously, too, and their maps break it down—all 214 Canadian miles of it—

to a sequence of mileage markers between put-ins and take-outs, supplies of drinking water and access to campgrounds. It's precisely eighty-eight miles of pleasant paddling from where the river comes up across the line to the town of Milk River, forty-five more to the provincial park at Writing-On-Stone. Between the town and the park, there are five places to start or finish a leisurely day trip, three of them with campsites, toilets and firewood.

In those forty-five miles, the river loses perhaps four hundred feet of elevation, enough to keep it moving smoothly, not so much as to create cataracts or rapids. Below the park, on the full eighty miles of the Milk that arches east and south through the great canyon and back to the border, there are just two bridges and the Pinhorn headquarters. There is no place to camp, no water, no firewood and no way off the river.

Still the paddlers come downstream from the park or the bridge at Aden. Most try it early, at the end of May or the beginning of June, hoping that the river will still be carrying late runoff to supplement the Montana-bound irrigation water. Even then, there will be snags and sandbars and bottom-scraping gravel banks. And there will be dead quiet and absolute isolation.

From down in the canyon, the world ends at the ragged rims, in places far enough apart to leave a half mile of sky. That is enough to give the blinding sun absolute access to every corner, baking the ground to rock and drawing its own share of the precious water up into the shimmering light. Slumping and collapsing down onto the broad floor, the walls are an impossible confusion of broken sediments, bizarre hoodoos and ragged side gorges that lead away around blind corners to narrow, mysterious places. Even in a country made of badlands, of deserts carved by water, the canyon of the Milk River has no equal. There is no other place that can match it for raw majesty, no other place that feels quite so lonely and quite so perfectly renders the illusion of things the way they used to be.

Were it anywhere else, the Milk River canyon would see an unbroken string of canoes and inflatables, wilderness camp-grounds and interpretive signage. There would be trails leading up to its huge stands of pure desert yucca, to the eagles' nests and the fords where the surveyors, the cattlemen and the boot-leggers crossed. And there would be a parking lot somewhere down near the border where second vehicles would await the voyagers and take them back to some nearby town like Medi-cine Hat. But raw geography and an invisible borderline con-spire to make all this impossible. Once paddlers pass the Pin-horn headquarters and drift down into the deepest, richest part of the canyon, there is no way out. Nothing short of a viola-tion of international law will get the paddlers back to the wider world.

The older guides make mention of a way out of the gorge. There was a rough ranch track that led down from Alberta 502, winding for miles through the low hills and skirting the rim before plunging down to an old Spencer cattle camp in the deepest recesses of the canyon. Constructed (if that's the word) for horse-drawn wagons, recommended only for serious 4x4s, it was a bad road in good weather, and in bad weather no road at all. Word is that even this perilous route has since slumped off its precarious perch to join the heaps of eroded rubble along the base of the canyon wall.

Those who look for the track and do not find it will be tempted to continue their search and stay with the river for a few more miles, looking for another way out. The next tracks they see will mean they have crossed into Montana and created for themselves a whole new set of problems. South of the line, neither the ranchers nor the border guards over at Wild Horse are even remotely amused by the appearance of accidental tourists.

Years ago now, the first concerted efforts of the preservation movement brought the high plains into a continent's consciousness, and there were great hopes for the Milk River country. The public's interest in its natural history grew as the interpretive programs at Writing-On-Stone were developed and the parks in the Cypress Hills began to draw more and more visitors. With all the new talk about ecosystems and the renewal of interest in the old, sensible idea of viewing entire watersheds as single, living entities, there were grand ideas floated about the Milk River country. There were faint hopes and wishful thinking that it might become some massive international park, encompassing in its most ambitious expression the remnant grasslands on both sides of the border, the Sweetgrass Hills, the river and its grand canyon, and almost everything else in between.

Somewhere in the dead record centers of at least four governments there are position papers and preliminary reports, but like most of the dreams which have fueled Milk River country, the hopes for preserving this land were doomed from the start. They were too grand, too ambitious and premature in their declaration that the huge pastures of wheat were on their way out. They were naive, too, in their assumption that surplus government money on either side of the border was more likely to put to the business of saving rather than damming the great canyon of the Milk. The dreams died in a declining economy.

Canada's federal government, though, still looking to make

a national park of some surviving shortgrass fragment, turned its attention east to Saskatchewan and settled on a three hundred and fifty square mile parcel along the border near Val Marie. Nothing was ever seriously contemplated by the U.S. government for Montana's Sweetgrass Hills. Any hope there might have been would have withered in the face of unwilling private ownership.

In Alberta, with the tiny exception of the Milk River Natural Area, there is no formal protection for what remains of the native grass or for the raw beauty of the canyon. The latest vision for the future of Alberta's natural landscape—Special Places 2000—recognizes nothing in the Milk River country as a special place, nothing that would be safe from the certain riches of new oil and gas production or from anything else that might promise new revenues for provincial coffers. Hopes have faded for a new highway to run west along the line of the Mounted Police march, connecting Fort Walsh, the Grasslands and Waterton national parks and bringing more visitors to the Cypress Hills and Writing-On-Stone along the way.

The highway has not been built, but the name Red Coat Trail appears on Alberta road maps. It's on a few signs along Saskatchewan's Highway 13 and on the eastern section of Alberta's 501, too, but the trail swings north to Highway 61, away from the Milk and away from where the Mounties really went.

Provincial officials have thought some about the old Spencer track into the great gorge, wondering if it can be made at least reasonably passable. It can't. They have looked at other places, too, hoping to find somewhere for a road to take the canoeists up from the river, but they are looking without a plan or a budget, and the eroding, unstable walls of the canyon will probably defeat them.

So what of the newest hopes for a country which thrives on breaking dreams? What will it take to shelter these last few fragments of the high plains shortgrass? As with everything else about this place, the answers to the questions lie buried in contradiction. It has been bred in our bones to see salvation in three readings and royal assent, to see the special places we have come to cherish defined by pages of complex legal terminology, by some impenetrable maze of legislated balance and counterbalance. But in protecting wild places while opening them to the wider world we seem so often to sow only the seeds of their own destruction. There are traffic jams in the heart of Yellowstone, three-year waiting lists to run the Colorado through the Grand Canyon and handfuls of pamphlets at every park gate outlining carefully what one must not do. The last hope must be that it will not happen here.

Those who have found this country will always be torn between the evangelical need to share its wonder and the knowledge that for all its horizon-stretching sprawl it is a delicate place. Though outsiders here are few and far between, a sight still rare enough to slow a rancher's pickup and draw a curious once-over, their numbers have been growing. In government offices across the province, brochures promoting the Milk River Natural Area, Red Rock Coulee and Writing-On-Stone stand side by side with those for the better-known Kananaskis and Cypress Hills parks. Newspapers and television news programs have been reporting more and more stories about the renewed efforts to save the swift fox and the burrowing owl and the ferruginous hawk, struggles centered on the Milk River country. The managers of the Pinhorn are seeing more boats in the canyon, and there are more and more canoes resting next to the tents at Writing-On-Stone. But in a land where a wagon track can remain visible for a century and a hiking boot can match a decade of erosion with a single scrape against the base of a hoodoo, it does not take much to leave a small scar or for those small scars to multiply into death by a thousand cuts.

What will protect the Milk River country will be the same pure truths that have always set it apart, the things that time and again conspired to make it the last place. Sheer distance and hard isolation will keep it as safe as anywhere can be. The main roads deliberately skirt the center of this country, and travelers will not find themselves here by accident. There is nothing but their own curiosity to lure them off their drive from Medicine Hat to Havre or Lethbridge to Great Falls. Not many will push on east beyond the turn-off to Writing-On-Stone. Few will be drawn to follow the gravel down from the cool, green summits of the Cypress Hills and out toward the dry, shimmering distance of the Sweetgrass. Few will ever come upon the Pinhorn, and fewer still will let its rough tracks lead them deep into its huge heart.

This dry, delicate place should always be hard to get to, always just beyond the reach of those who take their pleasures in the easy and the obvious. Infinitely wide and infinitely subtle, it is a country which calls for the telescope and the microscope in equal measure, building its immensity from numberless tiny details.

From the shoulder of the Sweetgrass Hills, the great sweep of the Milk River country is at once both comforting and daunting. Even with the impossible scale of it all, the roads and fences give it a benign, almost pastoral look. But come down from the hills and turn away from the roads, walk onto the Pinhorn or a mile into the Lost River badlands, stand face to the wind at the rim of the great canyon and the indifferent, primitive soul of this country comes pouring back, still wielding its enormous power to inspire and to humble. As long as it lives here in these fragments of an ancient infinity, there will be hope for this last lonely place.

BIBLIOGRAPHY

There are many books and articles which deal with the life and history of the Milk River country and its place in the larger world. Each adds something to an understanding of this unique part of North America. The following selection contains both those works which have informed this book in some substantive way and those which are highly recommended for further reading.

Alt, David and Donald W. Hyndman. *The Roadside Geology of Montana.* Missoula: Mountain Press Publishing, 1990.

Beaty, Chester B. *The Landscapes of Southern Alberta.* Lethbridge: The University of Lethbridge Printing Services, 1989.

Berry, Gerald L. *The Whoop-Up Trail.* Edmonton: Applied Art Products Ltd., 1953.

Breen, David H. *The Canadian Prairie West and the Ranching Frontier.* Toronto: University of Toronto Press, 1983.

DeVoto, Bernard. *Across the Wide Missouri.* Boston: Houghton Mifflin, 1975.

DeVoto, Bernard. *The Course of Empire.* Lincoln: University of Nebraska Press, 1983.

Duncan, Dayton. *Miles From Nowhere: Tales From America's Contemporary Frontier.* New York: Viking Penguin, 1993.

Duncan, Dayton. *Out West: An American Journey.* New York: Viking Penguin, 1987.

Francis, R. Douglas. *Images of the West: Changing Perceptions of the Prairies.* Saskatoon: Western Prairie Producer Books, 1989.

Gayton, Don. *The Wheatgrass Mechanism: Science and Imagination in the Western Canadian Landscape.* Saskatoon: Fifth House Publishers, 1992.

Graspointner, Andreas. *Archaeology and Ethno-history of the Milk River in Southern Alberta.* Calgary: Western Publishers, 1980.

Gray, James H. *Men Against the Desert.* Saskatoon, Western Prairie Producer Books, 1978.

Howard, Joseph Kinsey. *Montana: High, Wide and Handsome.* New Haven: Yale University Press, 1974.

Hume, Stephen. *Ghost Camps.* Edmonton: NeWest Publishers, 1989.

Jones, David C. *Empire of Dust.* Edmonton: University of Alberta Press, 1991.

Kittredge, William, ed. *Montana Spaces: Essays and Photographs in Celebration of Montana.* New York: Lyons & Burford, 1988.

Lavender, David. *Let Me Be Free: A Nez Perce Tragedy.* New York: Doubleday Anchor Books, 1992.

Lavender, David. *The Way to the Western Sea: Lewis and Clark Across the Continent.* New York: Doubleday Anchor Books, 1988.

MacGregor, James G. *Vision of an Ordered Land: The Story of the Dominion Land Survey.* Saskatoon: Western Prairie Producer Books, 1981.

Malone, M.P., R.B. Roeder and W. L. Lang. *Montana: A History of*

Two Centuries. Seattle: University of Washington Press, 1976.

McHugh, Tom. *The Time of the Buffalo*. Lincoln: University of Nebraska Press, 1979.

Melcher, Joan. *Watering Hole: A User's Guide to Montana Bars*. Helena: Montana Magazine, 1983.

Nelson, J.G. *The Last Refuge*. Montreal: Harvest House, 1973.

Parsons, John E. *West on the 49th Parallel: Red River to the Rockies*. New York: Wm. Morrow & Co., 1963.

Stegner, Wallace. *Beyond the Hundredth Meridian: John Wesley Powell and the Second Opening of the West*. New York: Penguin Books, 1992.

Stegner, Wallace. *Wolf Willow: A History, a Story and a Memory of the Last Plains Frontier*. New York: Penguin Books, 1990.

Webb, Walter Prescott. *The Great Plains*. Lincoln: University of Nebraska Press, 1981.

Welch, James with Paul Stekler. *Killing Custer*. New York: W.W. Norton, 1994.

Willock, Thomas. *A Prairie Coulee*. Edmonton: Lone Pine, 1990.

Willock, Thomas. *The Ecology of Fishes in the Missouri (Milk River) Drainage of Alberta*. Thesis, Carleton University, Ottawa, 1969.

The Royal Tyrrell Museum of Palaeontology. *The Land Before Us: The Making of Ancient Alberta*. Red Deer: Discovery Books, Red Deer College Press, 1994.

Quotations from James Doty are from Hugh Dempsey's article "A Visit to the Blackfoot Camp" (*Alberta History*, 14 [3]: 17026).

In 1980, Alberta commemorated her 75th Anniversary as a province. Communities were encouraged to produce local histories in celebration. Several Milk River country histories were published, and they offer a wealth of detailed, firsthand anecdotes, most of them written by those who first settled here. Among those worth consulting are: *Under Eight Flags: Milk River and District; Prairie Footprints: A History of Pendant d'Oreille; Manyberries Chinook: A History of the Communities of Glassford, Manyberries* [etc.] and *The Forgotten Corner: A History of the Communities of Comrey, Catchem* [etc.].

ABOUT THE AUTHOR

Tony Rees was born in Great Britain in 1948 and came to Canada in 1957. Educated at the University of Western Ontario, he holds an M.A. in 17th Century English Literature. Formerly Archivist—Fine Arts and Supervisor of the City of Toronto Archives, he moved west in 1981 to become the first City Archivist for the City of Calgary. He later served as records manager for the 1988 Calgary Winter Olympic Games and for seven years as Chief Archivist at Calgary's Glenbow Museum. Tony Rees lives in Calgary.